# A HISTORY OF ATHERTON

**By John Lunn**

**Edited by Peter Riley**

P & D RILEY

First Published 1971 by Atherton District Council

This edited edition first published 1994 by

P & D RILEY,
12 Bridgeway East,
Windmill Hill,
Ruuncorn,
Cheshire WA7 6LD



ISBN NO: 1 874712 10 7

## INTRODUCTION

In this, as in any edited book, there are drastic cuts forced upon the publishers for space reasons, therefore someone's ancestor, favourite church or other building, or some other part of the region's history, has had to be sacrificed. For this we can only apologise in advance but hope the cuts have not been too severe.

To publish a book of this kind, the original of which has been out of print for many years, it is sometimes only possible in an edited version to keep the selling price to a reasonable level, therefore allowing the ordinary people of Atherton to own at least one version of Lunn's work.

We realise that Lunn's work was first published more than 20 years ago and that many aspects of Atherton's history will have altered beyond recognition, including buildings and streets, and it is our wish that some enterprising local historian will come forward in the not too distant future to remedy the changes in a new history of the town. In the meantime, we sincerely hope readers anjoy this reissue of a classic local work.

PETER RILEY

1994

## ACKNOWLEDGEMENTS

The publishers wishes to thank Len Hudson of Wigan Heritage Service archives for supplying the photographs in this book and to Tony Ashcroft, Local Studies Officer, Leigh Library, for his help. Grateful thanks also to Alan Hulley of Chamleys Bookshop, Leigh, for his assistance and enthusiasm in this project.

# A HISTORY OF ATHERTON

## ATHERTON

The name of the township is derived from a Saxon word meaning little brook. It could equally be traced from the name of an indigenous tree, the alder, which singularly differentiates one of the principal houses of the township today—Alder House. The earliest spelling of the name was adurton, which is close enough to the Saxon adre. Atherton first becomes recorded in documents of the 13th century and takes on from then a general acceptance as a well-defined locality. The township was one of six vills comprising the parish of Leigh and the suffix ton indicates some cluster of dwellings, in all likelihood a stockade. Another township, Pennington, in the same parish is probably from the root name of the family older than Atherton. Chowbent as a rival topographical description comes later. The four other vills of the ancient parish have no trace of urban influence—Bedford, Westleigh, Tyldesley and Astley. The manor of Atherton maintained a purity of descent from the very first days of recorded time down to the present age. Earliest documented tenants of the manor were Norman and held their lands from the Botelers of Warrington, who were the king's tenants-in-chief. The Athertons owed feudal duties to them and were, judging from the early names of the family, Henry, William and John, of origin alien to the older race of Saxons. The military duty of the Botelers was to guard and maintain the bridge over the Mersey and supply the king with knights and men-at-arms, when called upon to do so. On great ceremonial occasions, such as the coronation, the Botelers poured out the wine for the king and royal guests.

## THE TOWN OF THE LITTLE BROOKS

Accepting the derivation of the place name as being the most probable there are seven streams which drain the area assigned to the Saxon town by the earliest surveyors. Water was a life necessity to early settlers and its availability essential in attracting human habitation. Hindsford brook, the natural boundary running with Shakerley was called, after a Saxon saint, Goderic brook. Chanters flowed in a meandering course through the valley and supplied power for the Lodge mill. In Bag Lane the stream there, which once had a platt, was known after the name of a local family as Knight's brook. Colliers brook drained the north upland area and like Knights derives from a local name. Small brook was a convenient natural landmark to divide off Westleigh, as was Westhoughton brook for the hamlet of Daisy Hillock. Red Waters brook was the seventh.

## HUGH ATHERTON, 1305

The Athertons were very numerous in these parts of south Lancashire. Some are found in Hindley and other nearby townships. Richard Shevington had land in that town, from which he took his name and complained that Hugh Atherton, Richard Shuttleworth, John Fairclough and his wife Maud had dispossessed him of some of his rights, but they had not put in any appearance in the royal court. On June 16, 1305, their attorney, Henry Legth appeared before the king at Chichester and gave assurance that they would answer to the writ, for the sheriff had seized their lands in default. Much later in the same century there is a case in 1330 heard at Lancaster in which Hugh Atherton the elder was in dispute with Henry son of William Atherton, Agnes late his wife and Alexander Atherton.

## THE ATHERTON FAMILY IN 1315

For a very long time the Athertons could always provide a male heir to take on the many duties which a landed feudal family had to perform. From the year 1315 and earlier right down to the death of mad Richard in 1726 direct descent failed only twice. William died without son to succeed in 1461, when his brother, the first of a long line of Johns, followed. The inheritance then carried through to 1628, when John Atherton passed the estates to his brother John, born of the second wife of his father; the male descent closed in 1726 with Richard Atherton, after five centuries of distinguished service to king and state as knights of the shire in parliament or in the foremost counsels of the county as sheriffs and in one case as sheriff of Durham. With the failure break of this long descent in 1726 there came daughters, who by marriage merged the Atherton estates with the family of Powys.

## MARGARET ATHERTON, 1323

Margaret was the daughter of William Atherton; she had become a creditor of Richard Hulton for the large sum of 200 marks, and there was difficulty in getting paid. To safeguard her claim Margaret took steps to have the debt engrossed on the Close Rolls of the king, with the added security that if he did not pay, the money could be levied on his goods and lands in county Lancaster.

## TAXES IN 1332

A tax was levied at Michaelmas 1332 by King Edward III on all moveables in Atherton and the sum accounted for by the collectors of West Derby hundred was 36*s.* 8*d.* Henry Atherton, lord of the manor, paid 8*s.* and his trade contemporary, Alexander Naylor, 2*s.* 8*d.* Altogether 11 men of the township were assessed to pay. The passage of time has made some of these names difficult to outline. One John Carpenter was a substantial builder, for his payment was as great as that of Henry Atherton. Another William Chapman was a trader at local fairs; his tax was 2*s.* 4*d.* Some of these men may not have been located in Atherton, but were trading from the town as a convenient point of operations.

## THE BATTLE OF CHADDOCKHURST, 1323

Lancashire was very disturbed wth civil war factions in the reign of Edward II. Armed men joined one or other leaders and rode across the country, robbing and breaking the peace. In January 1323, followers of William Bradshaw met those of Hugh Tyldesley at Chaddock Hall and a fight ensued. There were about 100 armed men on one side and 80 on the other; four were killed. Among the insurgents was Roger Atherton, a notorious disturber of the peace. He came with his brother Adam and joined in the battle. Later he was brought before the king at Wigan and fined 40*s*. for all his trespasses. Among his sureties for the payment of the fine was Henry Atherton.

## CATTLE STEALERS, 1333

The Hulton family was not popular locally: they were too acquisitive and ambitious. About this time Henry Atherton, Roger Atherton, son of William Atherton, and others from the township, including a carpenter and a cook, had joined a crowd of cattle stealers and had rounded up 18 oxen, 8 cows and 120 bullocks belonging to Adam Hulton at various places named as Westhoughton, Rumworth and Manchester. The malefactors had depastured Adam's crops and had mowed his grass. He took action against them and the case on July 16, 1333, was set down for hearing by the king's judges.

## ROYAL PARDON, 1361

Richard Atherton had committed many breaches of the king's peace and had joined the army for self-protection against punishment. During the campaign in France of 1361 he had rendered good service in the company of David Heaton and asked for his well-earned pardon. The king remitted all actions against him right up to the feast of Michaelmas 1360.

## A SERVANT OF HENRY ATHERTON OF HINDLEY, 1376

Outlawry was a grave punishment; it deprived a man of all his common law rights and his lands and moveables became the king's property. Henry Sale had so been deprived and the eschaetor had levied execution on the lands of Henry Sale in Bedford. He was son of William and claimed he was innocent. There were at least three other Henry Sales who could answer to the charges. These were identified as Henry Sale, Henry Sale, whose father was Richard, and Henry Sale, a servant of Henry Atherton of Hindley. The innocent Henry Sale had petitioned the king and the eschaetor of Lancashire was so informed.

## AGINCOURT, OCTOBER, 25, 1415

Two members of the Atherton family were present at this famous battle. They were William and Nicholas. According to the retinue rolls of the king, William Atherton, besides his own personal service about the safety of the king's life, furnished two foot archers. Nicholas was under greater expense; he brought two horse archers. William was 31 years of age in 1415. Nicholas was his cousin, son of his more famous father, the retainer of John of Gaunt.

## BEDLAM, 1437

On March 18 of that year the brothers and sisters of the hospital of St. Mary of Bethlehem by the walls of London were commanded to accept Edward Atherton, chaplain, as their warden. In this hospital were immured the unfortunate lunatics of that age and Atherton's description as chaplain discloses he was a member of the Church, but had not yet taken priest's orders. In 1438 he was given the benefice of Diss in the diocese of Norwich and the next year resigned the living of Stanford Rivers in Exeter. He died before 1457. In his career he had been an active pluralist and in 1436 was prebendary of the free chapel of St. Stephen within the Palace of Westminster.

## A ROSE RENT, 1440

On November 7, 1440, John Byrom leased to William Atherton, son and heir of William Atherton, knight, a field for ten years. The rent was a rose at Midsummer, "if demanded". The close rolls scribe called the field "Kekhalle Rydynge". It was the Kirkhall riding in Leigh.

## A COMMISSION ON PIRACY, 1470

A Genoese merchant, Ralph Vivaldis, had shipped to London 63 bales of woad. The king of England had given him a safe conduct for himself, crew and ship. While at anchor in the Thames evil men boarded the vessel and seized the bales. John Atherton esquire among others was one of a commission commanded by the king to detain a ship belonging to Robert Ros of Calais and arrest all persons guilty of this act of piracy.

## RIOT IN LEIGH CHURCHYARD, 1535

A warrant for the arrest of Thomas Pomfret, an Atherton carpenter, had been sent to the sheriff, Thomas Butler, who entrusted the execution of it to his undersheriff, Richard Penketh. He came to Leigh on Sunday after the Circumcision 1535 and found Pomfret and his two friends inside the church, where mass was being celebrated. They tried to arrest Pomfret and a riot occurred both inside and outside in the churchyard. The undersheriff and his posse were trying to take the men to Morley Hall in Astley, where they could be bound over to appear. John Atherton and Richard Atherton were present on this occasion and supported by a crowd of some 200 they entered the house of William Linley in Leigh where the undersheriff had taken refuge and broke the arrest. Those who were willing to go and act as sureties for Pomfret were William Choll, Robert Lilling, John Astley and John Alred, all Chowbent men. The case was later heard in the Duchy Court at Westminster. Pomfrets were living in Atherton for generations, some of them innkeepers.

## JOHN ATHERTON TO MR. RADCLIFF, 1560

John Atherton had been commanded by the earl of Derby on April 13, 1560, by order of the Lord Lieutenant of the North to levy a certain number of men of Cheshire. Radcliff was appointed to collect 8 archers with steel caps, lead malls, daggers, bows and arrows, all tall and lusty men, who were to concentrate at Leigh, 12 o'clock on Thursday, April 29, that Atherton might see how they were accoutred and certify the earl what had been done. This same Atherton had been included in the general pardon of the young queen. On the patent roll he is described as "John Atherton of Atherton or the Lodge alias of Chowbent alias Sir John Atherton sheriff of the County of Lancaster". The pardon was for all crimes and trespasses which he had committed. Many of the complaints and charges against him would arise out of the performance of his royal office. Atherton became a loyal supporter of the Elizabethan religious settlement and on July 20, 1562, was appointed on a commission headed by the earl of Derby and the bishop of Chester to suppress hostility to the policy of the queen and punish all opposition. Atherton's knighthood was by the Earl of Hertford in 1544, for service in the invasion of Scotland.

## A LUNATIC, 1567

Mary Ryder, whose husband William had died, was a lunatic. On February 6, 1567, William Atherton was appointed by letters patent to be her guardian. She held lands in Yorkshire and Atherton had to render strict accounts of income and expenditure to the royal court of Wards. If ever she recovered sanity her properties were to be restored to her. This William Atherton was the one mentioned on the patent rolls January 5, 1562, and who was perpetual rector of Corfe castle and granted on that day the chapel of Kingston in Bristol diocese, vacant by death. Atherton was a clerk in the royal service and able thereby to collect for himself these lucrative aside employments.

## ATHERTON TITHES, 1567

At the Reformation the greater tithes in Leigh parish, which had belonged to Erdbury Priory in Warwickshire passed ultimately to the family of Urmston in Westleigh. Many people resented paying tithes meant for the Church to lay persons and John Urmston had trouble in collection. To ease his burden in 1534 he rented to John Atherton for £8 a year the tithes of corn, pigs and geese in Atherton. On July 1, 1567, this grant of fee farm was renewed at the same rent to Sir John Atherton of Fryton in Yorkshire. The deed is still among the extensive Lilford muniments. Atherton paid a yearly rent of £8 but in good harvest would collect more from the tenants.

## THE NAIL TRADE

The manufacture of nails was an industry located in Atherton for at least 600 years. The tax list of 1332 gives Alexander Naylor as a heavy payer on the over-all value of his goods. Shakerley too was famous for smithies and nails. Coal outcrops were the main cause of the location of the industry in these parts. Iron had to be brought from Yorkshire and Derbyshire and was traded as tough or soft iron, string iron, brake iron, rod iron and other varieties, when Spanish or Irish iron began to come to Liverpool. Nails made in Chowbent were familiar in shape, though of different sizes, and all had the small head bar; the round type came with machine manufacture. The first step was to purify the iron, sometimes to blend it with steel for better quality, and pour into sand-lined block moulds or stocks. The trade embraced lath nails, slate nails, sparrow bills, stake nails, thatching nails, and harrow pins. Often in the same smithy ploughs, scythes and pruning bills were manufactured alongside the nails. Pack horses took the products to market towns such as Denbigh, Manchester, Clitheroe and Kendal. The chapmen would often arrange for them to be stored in great arks awaiting sale. There are one or two cases of nailors leaving the trade and becoming ironmongers, buying iron on a large scale and selling it to local smithies. In Chowbent a specialized name of rock was often given to the worksmithy. These were held on lease and inside the forge, bellows and anvils, with hammers, bores, pincers, files, chisels, knives, wedges and stone troughs to hold water for cooling down the heated ore. In 1633 the price of latt nails was per 1,000 11*d.*, for the same quantity of horseshoe nails 5*s.*, and single board nails 1*s.* 8*d.* The nail trade produced fortunes for many families in Atherton and their prosperity was in sharp contrast to that of men in the other five townships of the old Leigh parish.

## BONAVENTURA ASTLEY, 1602

The Astleys that hoary homestead in Far Atherton with the huge date figures of 1669 set in the gable wall strikes far back into history. Even here in this isolated corner of the township the nail industry had taken firm root. Bonaventura was buried at Leigh April 7, 1602, and the next day the funeral file accompanied his wife to the same grave. Worthy neighbours, James Makant, Simon and George Smith and Simon Mather joined together on that latter sad day to assess the value of Bonaventura's goods. Hammers, boards, iron wedges and other worklooms belonging to his nailor's trade were of a modest value of 10*s.* In the smithy were two weighs, one for iron, the other for nails. The bible he read was 6*s.* 8*d.* and altogether he was worth £64 14*s.* 5*d.* His peculiar name, alien in Chowbent tradition, marks the height of Italian influence and manners in the England of that day. In 1632 died John Astley, plain husbandman, whose most valuable asset was £30 of hay bought upon a bargain from John Pendlebury. He held leases in Langley meadow and in John Radborn's field. When he died his kinsman Peter owed him £3. Then in 1644 this Peter was overtaken by death and a ground lease for 17 years, set at the big valuation of £50 was his best possession. Peter loved to shoot; he had a birding piece and a cross bow priced 13*s.* Both these Astleys were husbandmen.

## THE SALE OF THE MANOR, 1609

There was a settlement of Atherton manor made on May 18, 1609, by John Atherton the younger. Thomas Ireland, his feudal suzerain, took two-thirds of the lands, the rents of a great number of named tenants and a right in common to two-thirds of the profits of the mills and mines. The third part was represented by the Lodge and the tenants of John Atherton the younger. A dispute had arisen between the parties and a decree had been enrolled in the Duchy Court at Westminster which issued a commission to the sheriff of Lancashire Edward Stanley and his deputy Peter Marsh to see that the decree was enforced. From the year 1609 to the final award there had been disputes between Ireland and Atherton.

## JAMES MAKANT'S COW HIRE, 1611

Makant's livelihood was in husbandry, but here he extended its scope by profits from loan and hire. Not of money, but of beasts. He raised a herd and hired out cows. He received a fixed sum per head and the hirer fed the animal and from the milk and cheese profits paid Makant his rent. In 1611, the year of his death, Makant had eleven cows out under such arrangements at Melling's house in Westhoughton, two at Henry Walkden's, a heifer at Richard Southworth's, others with Ralph Astley and Richard Southern, at Higginson's and Charles Hindley's and one in Shakerley. In the Park were feeding three more heifers. While on his home pastures he tended five milkers and a bull and four weaning calves. By this means he had made surplus money described picturesquely as yellow and white. For on June 26, 1611, in his house was £6 13*s.* 4*d.* of gold and £11 of silver. One investment was a bill of demise from John Atherton for £6, John Mores owed Makant 2*s.* for my lady, probably one from the manor, and Peter Thompson had not paid Makant for the edish which he had allowed him to rake. It was the late crop of hay.

## ARTHUR CHOWE, 1614

Chowe family gave their name to Chowbent. In the map of Alder Fold estate which minister J. J. Wright has reproduced in his story of Chowbent Chapel, Chowe's tenement is shown on the very edge of the Mort estate. It must have changed in use during the passage of centuries. And here in 1614 died Arthur Chowe, when it was a smithy and farm combined. Chowe's stock comprised 3 cows, 2 stirks, 3 calves and 4 pigs and in the smithy were worktools at £3 12*s.* and the total of everything just over £40. His friends the Astleys and the Hindleys certified this value. Then John Chowe died in July 1633. Edward Chowe was his kinsman, to whom he left the care of his children. John was husbandman with certain rights in Richard Astley's land and had as well a lease of Langley Meadow. He possessed among his list of items 6 slippings of yarn, but there is no mention of any looms. Edward the relative of John was buried at Leigh, September 26, 1671, and in his will mentions George Smith and Richard Astley, both nailors. His estate of £28 was valued by Richard Chowe. Some of his cattle were grazing on the Mickle field.

## WITHINGTONS, 1614

This ancient homestead lying to the north of Atherton was the hearth of the family of Withington, yeoman and nailors, combining both to maintain an enviable prosperity. In 1614 died here George Withington, worth in all £112 17*s.* 10*d.* He left as heirlooms the dishboard and dresser to the eldest son Nicholas; the wife was Margaret, other children, Henry, John and Margaret. Son-in-law John Hartley was supervisor to see the will properly carried out. On April 18 sad neighbours came to value his belongings, a silver spoon 2*s.* 6*d.*, nails and iron £5 14*s.*, and Richard Stocks of Chester owed him 8*s.* 10*d.* His stock in cattle came to £28 13*s.* 4*d.* and from husbandry came his main income. In 1644 Nicholas died. He had a wide activity range. He defended himself with a sword. To take his nails to the Chester mart he fed two mares, one white, one grey, accoutred with pack saddles, owlies and woonties. He kept a store of nails in Chester in a great ark and customers owed him 13*s.* In the smithy his worklooms and nails ready for sale came to £3 1*s.* 6*d.*, and in his sum total of assets of £107 3*s.* 11*d.* was a pair of scales for weighing gold and a clock at £1 6*s.* 8*d.* Many chowbenters owed him money for in his prosperity he had been a trusting friend. Widow

Hurst was one of his debtors, James Hatton, Edward Chow and two relatives Henry and Joseph Withington were others. He had made two bad investments of £7 10*s.* 8*d.*, without security and no hope of being paid. Sober and religious friends Giles Green, Roger Rigby, John Hatton and Gilbert Aldred by their combined advice valued his goods. Other Withingtons continually reappear in Atherton's history till quite late times. John Withington, nailor died in 1665. His wife was Elizabeth and a daughter of the same name, who had married Edward Green. He had given by agreement to this daughter an ample dowry, but £27 of it was still unpaid at the time of his death. Other daughters were Ann, wife of Richard Lythgoe, and Margaret, unmarried. A son Henry took a pair of looms and all its accessories to be found in the shop. Withington left in all £51 6*s.* 6*d.* In his grate and iron chimney he burned coal and cannel. Later in 1687 died John Withington, whose personal records are much decomposed, but from them it is clear he was a weaver with Manchester customers. There at the date of his death he had stocked 80 ends of white jeans worth £56 and 20 white ends of 15 yards valued at £15. In the shop at Chowbent were 4 more ends of jeans with a stock of yarn and weft valued at £6. Among his unusual possessions was a silver cup, with a spoon, a toaster and silver buttons. His total wealth was £256, of which £141 was represented by debts. His valuers claimed deductions of funeral expenses of £66 9*s.* 7*d.* from the full total. This was a high cost and the claim itself most unusual.

## THE COURT HOUSE CHAMBER UPON THE CHOWBENT, 1616

The legal business of Atherton manor was enacted in a court house at Chowbent, the most populous part of the township. Manorial officers were elected there, decrees made, orders for the good of the estate and tenants paid their rents to the steward sitting there. The court finds a mention in an indentured deed of great length of February 27, 1615. John Atherton son and heir apparent of John Atherton transferred a wide expanse of wood, field and sough and the rents of some 53 tenants all named with right of tithe, services and the decayed mill called the Hall Mill or Lower Mill, with its kiln for drying and its damsides. Two thirds of the manor were made over to Ireland, the overlord of Atherton and by equal transfer two-thirds of the court house went with the agreement and the perquisites of that share were assigned too. Other lordship rights were alienated, such as two parts of the coal mines, the commons and full liberty to use the lane from Chowbent to the Lodge and from the brook there to Hindsford bridge and the lane from Chowbent passing John Mann's cottage to the lordship of Hulton and the lane from Greenhall to Shakerley. Roger Bradshaw gentleman and John Holcroft yeoman were Atherton's attorneys to deliver these extensive properties to Ireland. Much later the court house disappeared and the business of manor and court transferred to the King's Head.

## LEASE OF AN OLD SMITHY, 1616

Margaret Smith had made a lease on August 1, 1581, of a house 3½ acres and 37 falls of land and an old smithy. When she died her son Gilbert paid £15 to renew it in 1616. John Atherton the father was now aged in years and Smith, a nailor, was not to start paying rent of 14*s*. per annum until after the death of his landlord. Smith was obliged to do all the usual services which included duchy boons. But if the tenant needed any warranty or assurance of his lease, Atherton was not to be expected to travel more than five miles to defend the lease.

## WINTER FUEL FROM TYLDESLEY MOSS, 1626

Simon Chow and his wife Alice came from Atherton to Tyldesley Moss on September 2 of this year and carried away turves belonging to Lambert Vickars of Tyldesley. They were valued at 2*d*. A nailor dwelling in Tyldesley saw them and because it was their custom to come often and take dried cut turf from the stacks he laid an information before the mayor of Wigan, Hugh Langshaw. He said that not only he had seen these two come several times, but many of his neighbours had done so and the value stolen came to a much greater sum. Tyldesley Moss lay at the foot of the Banks on the south side.

## INNKEEPERS, 1626

Atherton inns have played an important part in township history. In early times they were not known by inn signs of evocative names, but more homely, by the surname of the innkeeper and sometimes even by his christian name. Old Israels meant the Wheatsheaf. In 1626 the justices licensed eight innkeepers in Atherton, who were Anthony Green, William Darwell's wife, Edward Green, Thomas Smith, James Hatton, John Thorp, William Hurst and James Pomfret. Some of these names recur in later records, for the hostelry tended to become handed down over long years of prosperous tenure. But of these it is possible to assign only one to any of the known inns familiar to the traveller today. James Pomfret was at the Punch Bowl, succeeded later by Robert, who died in 1726 and to follow him Richard. To the Punch Bowl falls the distinction of being one of the oldest of the king's highway inns in Atherton town.

## HINDSFORD BRIDGE, 1628

Goderic brook was the ancient name of this stream which was made a natural boundary between two townships. The highway surveyors reported in this year that the bridge was dangerous. In the report to the justices they called it Hinforth bridge. Upon an inspection of the bridge it was decided to rebuild it in stone. There were still many good planks left over from the old bridge which the surveyors took to Mosley Common to use there.

## THE HARE AND THE GUN, 1630

James Thorp was a townsman, who liked to see himself reflected in the recognition of what was right and lawful. During Lent of this year he saw yeoman Richard Smith take a gun, the barrel a yard and a half in length, and shoot a hare. Smith asked him to take it to his house and skin it, and when this had been done he buried the pelt in Smith's orchard. Then Thorp reported all this and Smith was brought before a special sessions of the peace at Chowbent in May 1630. Thomas Ireland who was the justice before whom Smith appeared held the major part of the lordship of Atherton at this time.

## A BREAK ARREST, 1633

Nailor Henry Aldred owed money to Edward Hurst; he would not pay and on July 23, 1633, Hurst had him outlawed at Lancaster Castle. Later Henry Beardsworth came to Atherton to arrest him. He met with a hot encounter; for all the Aldred family, their wives as well, supported by nailor William Thorp and carpenter Peter Pomfret were there to welcome him armed with swords, knives, daggers and other weapons. They beat him up so much that his life was despaired of. Great terror was struck into the hearts of the king's subjects in Atherton.

## A LINEN WEAVER, 1635

Linen weaving was concentrated in Pennington; but there were isolated websters working in other townships, who were able to amass wealth from this lucrative trade. Such was Roger Thropp, or with the transposition of the "r", whereby his Norse name became the more general, Thorp. When he died he had saved £521 16*s*. 10*d*. To weave his cloth he used five pairs of looms and to take him to Manchester, where he kept a chest, he rode his bay mare. Trading debts alone came to £85 6*s*. 8*d*. and the hoard of cash in the house was £140 17*s*. 6*d*. Thorp had bought a new cupboard just before his death and this he said was an heirloom for the son James. The wife was Isabel and younger sons Thomas and Roger were to have chamber and bed "to come and go unto". One daughter Anne had married John Bradshaw. Items like a pack of wool £12 and yarn at £100 measure out the extensive capital outlay needed by him as linen weaver.

## JAMES GREEN, 1638

Green belonged to the fraternity of Chowbent nailors, He asked a kinsman, George Green of Hindley, to order his affairs, for there was some £118 17*s*. 4*d*., mostly ready money, in his house and he wished to see this harvest of his life's trade for the benefit of his wife Margaret and four daughters. But Green wrote a letter to Chester and asked to be excused. Although James was a nailor he possessed no nailing tools. He was too old to have followed his regular employment.

## JOHN SCHOLFIELD'S FUNERAL EXPENSES, 1638

Along the highway which led to their ancient home, the Scholfields had lived so long, that they legated their name to it and still today the lane perpetuates this vanished race. John Scholfield died in November 1638, a husbandman, whose kinswomen spun their white yarn and then wove it on two pairs of looms. In remote Atherton, far from the bustle of life, they lived and died and paid their mortuary to the lord of the manor. In earlier times this had been a chattel, but later custom changed it to the fixed sum of 6*s.* 8*d.* When his friends set prices on his stock, furniture and implements, they put down also not only the cost of his own funeral, which was 24*s.*, but that of his mother as well. Scholfield like most Chowbenters cherished his Bible. But in his list of debts due, the cost of the items of goods, the letters of administration and personal expenses of the bondsmen at Warrington had been left blank.

## A DISORDERLY HOUSE, 1639

Serious complaints had been preferred against an Atherton innkeeper. He was John Hurst, whose inn was reported as being managed in a lewd manner. Mrs. Shakerley passed on these complaints to the local justice. He sold ale on Sundays and in the night time. At Quarter Sessions he was bound over to be of civic behaviour in future. Henry Orret, corn dealer, and William Maken, carpenter, went surety for this in a sum each of £5.

## THE RICHEST WOMAN IN CHOWBENT, 1639

Elizabeth Makant, who died in this year was with £597 19*s.* 7*d.* under her control the most well-to-do woman in the township. She was able to lend to the manorial family itself, for she had loaned to Mistress Atherton £2 3*s.* 2*d.*, secured by pawning some pieces of the family plate. She was able to keep £40 of ready money in the house and six silver spoons as well. All her large fortune she passed on to her daughter, Jane Damville, and her two children. To watch over her investments, loans and bonds she nominated Charles Herle, parson of Winwick, William Vernon, the antiquary of Shakerley, and James Naylor of Rainford, as trustees. Even her clothes valued at £10 justified her high social status.

## THE SPEAKER OF THE HOUSE OF COMMONS, 1641

In February 1641 the Speaker commanded great John Atherton to convene all males over 18 in the old parish of Leigh and administer to each of them an oath of protestation, which would determine their line of action in the coming struggle between King and Parliament. The place was the parish church in Leigh and altogether in Atherton, including the constable of the township, John Bradshaw, 219 names are enrolled. Among the six townships at this time Atherton was the most populous. These surnames reveal an admixture of two races, Saxon and Norse. There were two Athertons, George and Richard, besides the great John, whose names are draped with the title of gent. Four Chows appear, twelve Aldreds, nine Thorps, five Withingtons, eleven Astleys, twelve Greens and twenty-one Smiths. These were the sturdy families of the valleys and brooks. Hope Mollinex is mentioned; he was prominent in his day. There was James Brown, a kinsman of Rebecca, also styled gent. But one who calls for special mention. He was James Thorp, for of the Chowbent men he stood alone in refusing to take the oath. Under the eye of the great John Atherton it needed courageous conviction to refuse to subscribe. When all the lists had been written up they were sent to the county Members of Parliament, Ralphe Ashton and Roger Kirkby.

## THE SKIRMISH AT CHOWBENT, DECEMBER 2, 1642

During the Civil War many tracts relative to happenings in other parts of the kingdom were printed. As such they were propaganda for either one side or the other. Thomas Jesland, who was not a local figure, wrote on the day above an account of the skirmish at Chowbent between Royalists and Roundheads and circulated in London a week later. The encounter took place on a Sunday, when tidings came to those going to church that the Earl of Derby was bearing down on Chowbent. The news spread fast and before 1 o'clock 3,000 horse and foot had gathered and this force drove back the earl and his troops to Leigh. Local horseriders pressed the Royalists as far back as Lowton common, where a stand was made. The battle was short and sharp and the Cavaliers put to rout. Some were killed and wounded and about 200 prisoners taken. Only three local Roundheads were wounded. Many Chowbent nailors took part in the battle and to be better prepared they made themselves bills and battle axes.

## A PRISONER OF PRINCE RUPERT, 1644

The great John Atherton, son of his namesake father, served in the Roundhead ranks. Forces of both King and Parliament criss-crossed the northern parts of the kingdom in endless marches and countermarches, plundering wherever they went. In a list of prisoners taken by Prince Rupert's men soon after the battle of Marston Moor in 1644 appears the name of John Atherton. He was the supporter of Cromwell, who made him High Sheriff.

## THE OLD BENT CHAPEL, 1645

During the turmoil and social upheaval of the Civil War there arose the old Bent chapel on the site near to the parish church of St. John. The building served as a place of Puritan worship to the year 1721, when Richard Atherton turned the congregation out. Dorning Rasbotham described it as a small brick edifice; Chowbent men built it and John Atherton provided the chancel. This evidence comes from the account of Leigh parish sent to the bishop of Chester in 1717. The vicar of Leigh at that time was George Ward, striving to exercise stricter parochial rights over the two chapels of Astley and Atherton. Ward told the bishop Chowbent chapel had never been consecrated and he described the minister in 1717 as a dissenting preacher. He further testified in his statement that by direction of the bishop he had sometimes preached there, read divine service and used a book of common prayer and a large Bible, which were in the chapel desk and which were used as often as he came to Atherton. Ward was pressing his claims over Astley chapel at the same time and Roger Seddon, the curate, encouraged by Thomas Mort, refused to help at the parish church and had to be ordered by the bishop. Ward finally subjugated Astley chapel, which was slowly brought into the fold of the state church. So was Atherton chapel, but as opposition here was much stronger, it needed ejectment in 1721, when Chowbent congregation built an entirely new chapel on different ground. This turn of events left the road clear for the old Bent chapel to become episcopalian, in contrast to Astley, where in later years there was tremendous dissension and litigation. In the early days of the chapel there were few baptisms and burials, for these rites were done at Leigh. No graveyard was attached to the old chapel and when Roger Thorp made his will he desired to be buried inside the building. Only two baptisms are recorded at the chapel just after its foundation, proof that it was mainly used for prayer and sermon.

## THE GREAT CIVIL WAR, 1648

In the struggle between King and Parliament money and finance heavily harassed both sides and with the victory of the Roundheads there was a great shift of property and income away from the Royalists to the all-powerful commissioners. Atherton was enthusiastic for Parliament, the great John Atherton saw to that, but on July 14, 1648, an imperious order was handed to the constables of the town warning them of their peril. They would be sent to Lancaster prison if they did not pay their taxes to Colonel Egerton or give sufficient surety.

## A SEAT IN THE OLD BENT CHAPEL, 1653

The small brick edifice, the first chapel in Atherton was built in 1645; many sturdy Chowbenters made substantial gifts towards its erection and gave legacies to pay for the stipend of a minister. On September 13 Roger Thorp signed his will and asked to be buried "under the seate and form where I usually sit within the Chappell of Atherton". In these times under the Protectorate there was much breakaway from the traditional usage of the church and marriages were performed before magistrates or in public houses and baptisms and funerals took place at the chapels of Atherton and Astley in derogation of the rights of the mother church at Leigh. So Thorp in these lax times expressed his preference for the small brick edifice as a last place of peace. Not till October 1663 was his will proved, when the restoration of old authority was complete. He was a nailor, working in his own smithy and keeping a few farmyard animals for the family needs. He possessed a branding iron with his name embossed, so that he could letter his ownership on the many tools he possessed. In his low-eaved house was a clock, 12 spoons, a tin plate, throne pan, lantern and cresset to overcome the dark. His wife was Joan and his son and heir John. All his enumerated assets came to £86 16*d.* 2*d.*

## CHOWBENT SCHOOL, 1656

Chowbent's grammar school like the Bent chapel was set up in the troubles of the civil wars and probably located near to the meeting place of the Presbyterians. It was certainly established in 1656, when Richard Jolly was master. In 1668 Mr. Taylor was in office and the school flourishing. Four boys—Richard Hatton, Thomas Stockton, Thomas Seddon, and Nathaniel Lommax—went from the little school to Cambridge. Stockton became M.A. of Christ's College in 1671; he died young, for he was buried September 12, 1681, and described as minister of the Gospel. Hatton became vicar of Deane 1673–1711. Seddon was instituted rector of East Wittering near Chichester and in 1680 was vicar of Sidlesham. Lommax on February 25, 1686, entered the nonconformist academy of Calton and the careers of these old scholars of Chowbent school reveal today the success it had built up. In 1727 James Ranicars was master at the school nominated by William Rawsthorne and George Farington, executors of the will of Richard Atherton and guardians of his young daughter Elizabeth, which is evidence that the Athertons had a close connection with the old foundation.

## IN THE STOCKS, 1656

Punishment in the stocks was a summary on-the-spot type of method used to deal with offenders like drunks and vagrants. These once familiar features of village landscape have almost disappeared, except as proof of antiquity in isolated hamlets. Yet the term "laughing stocks" still lingers on, an enrichment of ordinary-day language derived from this type of effective punishment devised to suit the need of past generations. The constables seized the offender, set his feet in the holes, locked the boards and left ridicule by wayfarers to complete the irksome discomfort which ensued. On frosty nights a bucket of fire would burn near the feet, bought and carried there by a friend of the prisoner, or on hot summer days a tankard of ale. The Chowbent stocks were placed in front of the small brick edifice, the meeting house of sober citizens, who resorted there on the Sabbath. During the rule of Cromwell a high religious tone suffused society and swearing, drunkenness and refusal to go to church were frowned upon. Robert Heyes of Chowbent had sworn two wicked oaths, when drunk, and was fined 15*s*. which was to go to the poor rate. Henry Smith for the same misdemeanours, 10*s*. but he escaped paying by fleeing his country. James Thropp went one better; he swore three oaths, but having neither money nor goods, he was put in the stocks for 15 hours. After a stretch of 11 hours he collapsed, fell sick and was unable to sit his sentence out, because he was an old man. On August 13, 1656, Thomas Holcroft was very drunk and swore four wicked and profane oaths, for which the constables of Atherton fined him 28*s.* 4*d.*; he had neither money nor goods and in consequence was set in the stocks for the very long stretch of 27 hours.

## THE OFFICE OF CONSTABLE, 1662

No one liked this unpopular office, with its dangerous tasks, its night watch and ward. Yet if elected at the local hustings the townsman had to assume his duty. In 1661 George Smith was put in office and took the usual oath faithfully to administer the duties before Justice Rawsthorne. Later on in 1662 John Hindley was acting constable and because of nonpayment of rates he had distrained on some goods of Mr. Holcroft, who sued him and Hindley lost the case. This cost him £3 10*s.* 6*d.* and he had to ask the bench of justices for a reimbursement order. He was successful in his petition and his successor was ordered to levy that extra amount of money and pay over to him.

## THE HOUSE OF CORRECTION, 1662

Susan Smith had been sent to the house of correction, because she brought into the world a non-wedlock child. Her sentence was six months. Her mother, Dorothy Smith, was very aged and oppressed with the bitterness of extreme poverty. But she worked and was able to pay for a bed in prison for her daughter and to look after her other children. It proved too much and her petition to the justices in 1662 pleaded that unless the daughter was enlarged and set free, her mother bade likely to become a burden on the town of Atherton.

## THE TANNER, 1663

There were a few who in the ancient parish of Leigh followed this trade, but the capital outlay was substantial. James Greenhalgh was tanner in the year 1658 and when he had processed his varied hides he sold them in Bolton, where much later a thriving tanning industry grew up. To tan the many skins he had to purchase bark. This alone accounted for £27 10*s.* Around his home were the shallow pits filled with lime and bark. In the lime pits were 13*s*. value of hides and 15 hides lying in bark were priced 50*s*. Stored away in the back part of his house were (with their market values): 17 upper leathers (£12 5*s*. 4*d*.) 5 peech hides (£4) 55 additional uppers (£37 6*s*. 8*d*.). Twenty-two calf skins, 5 kixs, 1 stirk skin, 7 horse hides and 11 dried peech hides all came to £11 1*s*. 0*d*. The bark mill with all its implements was only 13*s*. 4*d*. and the stock of lime 3*s*. Withal he lived well, a feather bed he slept on, honey from his two hives and eggs from his poultry. In the ancient hearth was a lanthorn and to tell him the hour of day a wooden watch.

## THE ATHERTONS' COAT OF ARMS, 1664

Lawrence Rawsthorne, the stepfather of the 8-year-old Richard Atherton, was summoned in 1664 by the great historian Dugdale, the Norroy King of Arms, to justify the Atherton claim to a coat of arms. Rawsthorne produced a pedigree which showed a continuous line of descent from Robert Atherton, sheriff of Lancaster in the time of King John to the present minor, Richard. The device was particularized as three sparrowhawks of silver on a red shield with a silver swan for crest. Such a coat harks back to the days of the great forests with abundant game and wild life and the right of the manor lords to hunt. There is one error in Rawsthorne's pedigree. John Atherton who died in 1617 married for his second wife a daughter of John Calveley of Saughton in Cheshire. The return gives Raphe.

## APPRENTICES IN THE NAIL TRADE, 1667

Poor and destitute children in Atherton were apprenticed to nailors, just as in later times cotton spinners admitted them to work in the dark mills and save the cost of bringing them up on the poor rate. Robert France, an orphan of dead nailor George France, was apprenticed by his uncle John, a clothier, to learn the art of nailmaking. The length of service varied from 4 years to 7, and could be longer. Nailmaking was a guild mystery, with its special rules governing the admission to the craft, the quality of wares and the service conditions of the young apprentices.

According to the will of Ellis Astley of Shakerley in 1584, the apprentice on shedding his indentures received 6*s.* 8*d.* from his master and a piece of iron. They were the guild's rules to regulate the setting up of a new member of the ancient craft. Printshop Lane in Hindsford is "apprentice shop", but this survival belongs to the history of the cotton trade.

## HEARTH TAX, 1667

This troublesome tax was based on the number of hearths in a house much in the same style as the window tax. John Seddon of Atherton had refused to pay his assessment raised on him by the inspectors of hearths and his moveables had been seized upon and detained. He in company with others complained to the justices, who referred the matter for hearing by two of their number.

## IN LANCASTER GAOL, 1677

Daniel Asken had lain in the dungeons of the castle for seven months on a committal order from the local justice, William Hulton, for Margery Orwell of Atherton had accused him of being the father of her child and as he could give no security to save the town hardship and the poor rate having to keep it he was sent to prison. For seven months nothing had been done and the child had not been legally filiated on him. He petitioned for an order for his release.

## LOCAL BRIDGES, 1670

Bridges on the main roads were a continual source of trouble to the local supervisors of the highways. Early structures were of wood and when the timbers decayed, the bridge became unsafe. As time went on, stone replaced wood as the accepted material, but the width was usually one carriageway. In 1670 Lawrence Rawsthorne was asked by the Bench at Wigan to view and inspect four local bridges in Atherton—Hoar Orchard Bridge, Hindsford Bridge, How Bridge and Stockplatt Bridge—and report his opinion as to what the cost would be to repair them. Stockplatt carried the road from Atherton to Leigh near to the church.

## CRABTREE FARM, 1670

At one time in domestic history crab trees were so appreciated that local folk regarded them like heirlooms and left them in their wills. This very ancient home stood in Crabtree Lane and yeoman William Smith who died in 1670 had taken a lease of land, identified as one mead two crofts and a pingle of Crabtree farm. At his death the lease had still five years to run and Smith had let Adam Twiss occupy the house and ground. Adam paid rent of £4 17*s.* 0*d.* a year and was to do all boons, and pay the leys and taxes. This five-year lease of Crabtree farm was worth in capital value £18. Smith was able to leave £65 0*s.* 4*d.* The income of the rent was shared by the widow Ann and Adam Twiss, and in case of failure to his sisters Elizabeth and Susan. One curious feature of the will was that Smith gave John Lever, curate at Leigh church, 2*s.* 8*d.* a year to augment his wages, but only so long as he stayed there. Yet in spite of the benefits Smith conferred, Adam and the other executor would not meddle with the business "considering the trouble it may bring upon us". So they renounced by letter to Chester.

## BLACKSMITH ADAM SALE, 1672

Adam Sale was the blacksmith of Chowbent in that longspent age when the horse dominated all transport on land. One would expect his smithy to be somewhere on one of the principal roads and in the centre of the community he served. Sales were long resident in Atherton. Besides shoeing horses he repaired cart wheels and made fellies. Around his small house roamed pigs and when he died he had stocked his larder with 78 lb. of bacon priced 3*d.* per lb., besides swine grease and cheeses. In the smithy were two stidges valued at £4, two great hammers and four hand hammers, two bellows, two hand rife files and his box of tools. He was widower when he died with Thomas, Cicely and Margaret, his children. Hope Molyneux and Henry Worthington were asked to witness his will, when he disposed of £97 16*s.* 3*d.*, the sum total of his long years of toil.

## RICHARD ATHERTON, CURATE, 1682

He was curate at the parish church in Leigh about the year 1674 and was buried there August 20, 1682. Whether he was connected with the landed family of the Athertons, so far no record shows.

## THE BEDSTOCKS IN THE FAR END OF THE CHAMBER, 1672

Beds, bedsteads, fourposters, truckle beds and feather beds were popular pieces of gifts. William Smith died in this year and described a bedstead as "in the far end of the chamber" and it was to be given to his son John. The wife was Ginnett and other children James, Katharine and Ginnett. Two of these were very young when the father died and their share of the £80 16*s.* 1*d.* he had won by his thrift was to be increased by £2 each to help them the better to battle with life. One unusual tool in his house was a marl pick and in the buttery was a pearl box. The family burned coal in three iron grates, bought it from the pit auditor and heaved it home in a coal cart. They lived daily on oatmeal, milk and cheese.

## ROADS IN ATHERTON, 1676

The surveyors of the highways, or as the report in the sessions papers says the "coseywayes", made in this year a full and complete survey of all those lanes which were not of the statutory width of 8 yards. None of the roads at this time had names given to them; they were referred to by the names of the frontagers. A full copy of the survey is given later.

## A DEFIANT SPINSTER, 1677

Spinster Margery Astley otherwise Aldred came to live in Atherton. The overseers of the poor took note of her arrival and reported the details to the local justice, William Hulton. They swore that she came on November 16, 1676, and that she had not qualified in any way for a settlement in their township. The matter was referred to the Ormskirk Sessions, where there was given a stern direction that the woman was to be sent to the House of Correction if she did not return to Tyldesley, where she was last settled.

## LAMBERT SALE'S LEGACIES TO HIS MAIDSERVANTS, 1677

Lambert belonged to that ancient family of Chowbent Sales, long identified with the best traditions of the neighbourhood. He was a substantial yeoman farmer, with a herd of 11 cows, one of which was lame. To each he had given a name, Petite Heffer, Lowton, Blackface, Brokenhorn, Wuldpie. The home where he lived was substantial and one of its rooms was called the Hall. In it they found 16 lb. of towe and 6 slippings of yarn, 2 books, 5 white plates and a looking-glass. In the farmyard ambled 15 geese. His wife had died before him and all her woollen clothes he gave to her sisters, Sarah and Catherine. His mother-in-law was to have her best hat. Then he remembered his two maids and gave them a handkerchief apiece "one of the best my wife did usually ware, the older servant to make her choice first". Sale by his great thrift was able to leave £259 9*s.* 4*d.*

## SWINEY LANE, 1678

Swiney Lane had been declared too narrow and an order made for the road to be widened. The Atherton surveyors were commanded to appear at Quarter Sessions and produce an account of the money collected for this purpose and pay William Ashton his costs.

## HOWE BRIDGE, 1679

Howe or hough meant a brow or bent and Howe Bridge as a place name finds a mention in this year, when a family by the name of Hulton lived here. In 1698 John Pickup of the Howbridge passed the title of his house to Thomas Bridge, whose family lived in the near locality for many a long year and who gave their name to Bridge farm. Pickup was a husbandman, leaving £52 3*s.* 4*d.* He fed nine cattle, some turning two to three years old and one pig and in "ye body" of his house was a table and clock.

## DISORDERLY PUBLIC HOUSE, 1681

Someone had complained to the justices that James Hatton and Richard Houghton, alehousekeepers, were men of evil behaviour. On Sabbath days discord prevailed for the most part of the time in their houses; persons were entertained there and goods bought and sold, contrary to the laws of the realm. The constables of Atherton were ordered forthwith to pull down their inn signs and charge them to stop keeping an alehouse.

## COAL RIGHTS IN 1616

The Athertons owed allegiance to the lords of Warrington. John Atherton married a daughter of his feudal chief and through this union the Athertons acquired Bewsey estates. All the complicated structure of a society, which had been made soon after the Norman Conquest was simplified, for the land and rights of the tenant-in-chief became those of his underlord in Atherton. In 1616 Thomas Ireland, who had succeeded to the Botelers, granted a lease to Nicholas Withington, Jane his wife, Margaret his mother, George, John and Jane, the children, for 90 years, if the lives could extend that far. There was paid a fine of £15 and the yearly rent of £1 6*s.* 11*d.* payable in three instalments at Michaelmas, Pentecost and the Purification. Additional one day's work at sheep shearing and one day filling manure. If the rent fell unpaid, Ireland's agent could drive any of Withington's cattle to the pound and finally could re-enter. But Withington had no right to get coal, cannel or slate or any other mineral. Ireland had the sole undisputed right to mine, make soughs, win and carry away coal with carts, wains and horses. Provided Withington performed all his obligations he could enjoy quiet possession without let or hindrance from Thomas Ireland, John Atherton the elder or John Atherton the younger. He had to attend the court of Ireland, whether held in Leigh or Atherton and was subject to the mill rights of the lord claimed by Ireland in Atherton or Leigh. This mill was the one in Old Hall Mill Lane and not the one at the Lodge. After the marriage of John Atherton with the daughter of Ireland the feudal rights attached to the Old Hall and its mill, court and pound merged with those of the Lodge in one tenure. This event was unique in local history. Elsewhere in neighbouring manors, a rival hall became so important that in course of time it assumed certain trappings of dignity, built a mill, established a pseudo-court and became a reputed manor.

Above: Old Atherton fire brigade

Below and overleaf: Coal pickers in Atherton

## THE ALEHOUSEKEEPER, 1682

Inns and taverns were not given distinguishing names in Chowbent until very late times. Thomas Hilton was one of the early tavern hosts and well known in the neighbourhood, where sometimes there came the better class of customer like the steward of the Atherton lands, Cowper, or Thomas Stockton, a well-to-do chapman. Both these one day came to witness his will and were asked to help the daughter, Mary, after her father's death. In the tavern there was a weight of 81 lb. of pewter, settles to sit upon and three-footed stools. One chest he owned was padlocked and to brew the ale he needed a lead pan with a cover. Elizabeth, another daughter, had married Thomas Mather of Pennington and a third, Anne, had died. Mary was to take this dead sister's clothes. Hilton's own worser suit was given to his brother-in-law, George Hatton. The total estate was £50 9*s*. 6*d*.

## CHOWS COTTAGE, 1683

William Aldred lived at Chows Cottage; he had leases of three other houses tenanted by Ralph Smith, Adam Sale and Robert Tonge. Tonge's was at Chowbent end. He gave the interest in all these to his brother-in-law Richard Holland till his son was 21. Holland had married Jennet, Aldred's sister. But Holland and Thomas Dunster, who both benefited by the terms of the will refused to meddle with it. Aldred had furniture in some of these tenants' houses, a table at Tonge's and three boards and at William Mather's a table, chimney, crow and chest. One room in the house where he died was known as the Long Room. He told the time by a brass clock, which was part of his total wealth at £69 6*s*. 4*d*.

## HOWE BRIDGE, 1685

The highways surveyors in this year, John Case, Ellis Makant and John Morris, viewed the bridge and because of its decayed condition asked for a grant of £20. But on reflection, they thought it better to pull the entire structure down and rebuild. Masons and workmen gave an opinion that the revised cost would be £25. At the Sessions the justices of the bench proved very generous and allowed £10 more, but the surveyors had to acquaint Sir Richard Atherton and Justice Hulton or any person appointed by the Court as to their final outlay of money.

## "AND TWELVE NAILORS SHALL CARRY ME TO MY GRAVE", 1684

Margaret Astley, living in deep isolation in far Atherton was widow of Simon, nailor. She died in 1684 and wished to be buried at Winwick. Twelve Chowbent nailors received 1*s.* each for bearing her body to the grave. As she gave 10*s.* to the poor of Lowton, this is some evidence of having come from there and Lowton was in Winwick parish. She gave a like sum to the needy in Atherton. George Astley was her son and to his son, a grandchild, she left a standing bed. There were numerous bequests to the Greens of Pennington, a meal ark for James Green's wife. Her clothes were set down at £7, which measures their fashionable elegance across the passage of centuries. She disposed of them with precision care, a red damsull to her step-son's wife, a new petticoat to Martha Turner, an old cloth gown to Ann Astley, her gown and best petticoat to Peter Leadbetter's wife. Simon the husband had died in 1681 and her dowry was £28 and a bed. But the bed never came to far Atherton; it stayed all the time at a brother-in-law's in Lowton. Astley's was an ample and great house, with kitchen, firehouse, middlemost chamber, highest chamber, buttery with room over, smithy with its great anvil, bellows, hammer, coals and tools. From the rafters hung 82 lb. of flitch bacon sides and a clock in a case ticked away the time. Near the smithy was the shop with three spinning wheels and £17 10*s.* worth of yarn. By three livelihoods these Astleys sustained their solid independence.

## THE LINENWEBSTER, 1687

Linen weaving was not one of Atherton's old industries, but John Platt of Chowbent made it his livelihood. He asked his executors to arrange with Sir Richard Atherton for a lease of his house to his son John, and if he died then for the daughters, Ann, Alice, Elizabeth and Mary. With John Platt lived an old woman, whose one cow, hay and household stuff was strangely included in Platt's total of £128 15*s.* 6*d.* An earlier John Platt had made his will in 1658. He was father of the son, who died in 1687 with Ann as wife. No one bothered to attend to his affairs, because of the troublous political times, till 1684, when court and family combined to get some order out of them.

## ROAD REPAIRS, 1685

It was customary for each frontager of the highways to keep his length in good repair and the elected surveyors of the township forced tenants to keep such stretches from becoming dangerous and a nuisance. This practice had been honoured in Atherton from time out of memory and a tenant could be fined by the steward of the lord's court if he did not comply in this matter of road repairs, while at quarter sessions the whole body of inhabitants for such neglect was sometimes indicted and heavily punished. In April 1685 a petition signed by 41 Chowbenters argued against a change of practice imposed by statute, which created out of the leys and rates a common stock of money to meet the repairs of the coseyways irrespective of any length, short or long. This did not accord with Chowbent wisdom; the objectors argued that the old system had worked well for over 100 years, since each man knew his own proportion to keep good and it penalized those who maintained their parts in repair and now they saw themselves forced to carry equal charges with those which were in great decay. The argument appears to have failed. In 1702 a second attack was directed against the common stock of money. Several townsmen sent a petition to the sessions, on which time has worn away most of the names. They contended for the new practice, as the hiring of frames and day labourers was a loss to the town, for the frames lay dormant and unused for long periods, the surveyors kept bad accounts and sometimes by undertaking the work themselves made money. The petitioners hoped in future such mistakes could be rectified and the common stock of money bring about peace and harmony. The names that time has not worn away which can still be read are George Makant, Henry Bolton, John Greene and Samuel Stockton.

## RICHARD HILTON TO PARSON WOOD, 1690

Hilton was typical of his age, a worthy Puritan, who came to the Chowbent and Wigan meeting houses of prayer. He left the sum of 40*s*. to Mr. James Wood, the elder of Chowbent and the same sum to the officiating minister at Wigan. These recurrent gifts of money index today the high esteem in which all three of the Wood ministers must have been held by the folk they served.

## GAOLED FOR WITCHCRAFT, 1689

Mary Carley's husband had been sent to prison for practising witchcraft and sorcery and was held at Lancaster Castle. The wife, left in Chowbent, had three small children to feed, the eldest being 4 years of age. She herself had a legal settlement in Rumworth and as they were all starving, she asked the justices for an order that Rumworth should support her and the children. Later, about the turn of the century, Katharine Walkden, very old, was accused of being a witch. She was examined by one of the Hultons at Hulton Hall and sent for trial, but she died at the Castle before she could answer to the charge.

## CHOWBENT CHAPEL, JULY 29, 1689

An Act of Parliament in this year required dissenters to secure a licence from Quarter Sessions to use any building for public worship. These members of the Chowbent congregation—John Rigby, Henry Withington, John Hartley and John Astley—signed the petition and described the building as a "certaine Chappell in Atherton comonly called Chowbent Chappell". This document of great importance proves that the meeting house was used by dissenters for public and divine worship, whatever the claim of a vicar of Leigh might have been, when he wrote in 1717 that he sometimes preached there and that a book of common prayer was kept in the desk for his use.

## THE CHOWBENT WATCH, 1690

Moses Bradley, a vagrant Irishman, with no means of subsistence had been arrested by the watch in Winwick and by them conveyed as far as Chowbent, where they left him. Here the Chowbent watch apprehended him and Thomas Marsh, one of the constables, took him before Mr. Hulton, a justice of the peace, who signed a mittimus and sent him to gaol at Lancaster. The constable then asked for the cost of taking him there and that Winwick, in that they had made the first arrest, be ordered to pay this. The watch house was situated on the Chowbent: it was a focal landmark for the constables to meet there and detain persons committed to the sessions, the houses of correction or Lancaster Castle. In 1692 there is an entry of *4d.* for putting in a new grate and the cost of coal for heating the watch house came from the rates.

## THE WAR AGAINST LOUIS XIV, 1691

Atherton taxpayers made heavy contributions towards the vigorous conduct of the war in the Low Countries against France. Double taxes of *4s.* in the £ were frequently levied on all property. Each quarter the collectors paid sums of £9 for the years 1691–6 to the war expenses. This was almost £40 a year additional to the other leys and taxes which the town had to find for the normal running costs of local government.

## THE WORKHOUSE, 1692

At this period Atherton shared with Pennington the cost of supporting a pauper house. This building was rented and Atherton's share of the annual rent was £1 *5s.* Poor and destitute persons were sent there by the overseers. From the great number of informative records which have survived, a full picture of life and conditions inside can be pieced together. Children were clothed with smocks and shod with clogs (these cost *8d.* per pair), and when they attended school, the rates paid for their school money. The number of inmates varied from week to week. A random choice shows in September 1748 some 70 persons there, average cost of upkeep per head 15¾*d.* Anyone capable of gainful employment had to work inside or be sent outside to such persons who asked for casual labour. Often what was "gotten" by them exceeded the cost of individual keep. James Smith earned a high sum of *19s.* in one week, which helped to reduce the rates. And in the same accounts for 1748 Halliwell's lad brought in *3s.* and Halliwell's wife *3s. 6d.* There was a loom shop attached to the poorhouse and Thomas Hasleden rented a rock or smithy to the overseers in Leigh where the Atherton nailors could make nails. Repeated purchases of thread and inkle or coarse tape were for making up materials and heald yarn was provided for those set to spin. Inmates were fed on wholesome meal and old men had the solace of tobacco to smoke or chew. Burial cost of a dead pauper as shown by the note on Peter Flitcroft in 1749 was 13*s*. 2*d*., but drink at the funeral cost 2*s*. 6*d*. A shilling was the general charge for laying out a corpse and 2*d*. for drawing a tooth. At regular intervals the barber came to trim and shave. In the governor's accounts are items such as sulphur, bellows, laces, birch besoms and brushes.

## HOUSE AND GROUND RENT, 1690

Chowbent houses were formerly held on three-lives leases and when two lives had fallen in, the survivor had to pay a heavy sum to the Athertons to have one or more additional lives inserted in the lease. Such tenures were uncertain and a fixed term of 99 years replaced them. Carpenter Hugh Brobbin died in 1690 and his rent for house and patch of ground was £4 a year. On it he could pasture two cows and sow a part with corn. By this means he could hardly starve and he could always implement the family household budget by his carpentry and his wife could always turn to spinning. The stock of timber at his house was valued at £7 and in yarn there was 8*s*. 4*d*. One unusual item he owned was a tackener, besides a watch and books.

## MEDICAL CARE UNDER THE POOR LAW, 1692

Care of the sick and aged was an important part of social poor law administration and in Atherton, except for one case reported on the Quarter Sessions papers, the overseers were often considerate and humane. Timothy Seddon had been hurt in a coal pit in 1751. He was cared for by Dr. Morton, who sent in a bill for 10 guineas; it was a large sum. Yet it was paid. A local practitioner attended the poor patient and prescribed medicine for him. At the end of the period a note was sent in for the overseer to include with his accounts. William Aldred in 1740 was attending some 41 sick persons unable to pay themselves. His charges and those of others like Dr. Guest of Pennington forced up the poor rate levy. Charges they made were for leeches, febrifuge powders, pills, pectoral tincture, anodines, Jesuit's bark, purging salts, catarall pills, Julap astringent, pectoral linctus and balsam, all set down with great care on long sheets of columned paper.

# OVERSEERS OF THE POOR, 1692

Very full and illuminating details of the Atherton overseers of the poor begin in 1692 and continue to 1840. To collect the poor rate two officers were appointed, one for the town's higher side and one for the lower. They received pay for their work and in the early period the annual payment was £4, plus expenses, such as horse hire and turnpike dues. But the office was a time-consuming one, many journeys to make on public business often to distant places. If a case of settlement came up, this would entail a journey to where the justices of the peace were in session in order to get a decision. Sometimes an overseer continued in office for several years. Edward Green, James Hope and John Baxter did so, electing at times to deputize for others whose turn it was to act. These full and numerous accounts are loose slips of paper attached to the balance for the year of office, then posted up and examined and signed by other ratepayers of the town, usually at the annual meeting. In 1714 no less a person than Thomas Bridge, the maltster, took office for the lower side. The amount of rate collected varied from year to year. In 1697 it was £31 17*s.* 5*d.*; by 1740 it was £154. An overseer needed to be a man of acumen and business. John Gregory was not fond of work, when overseer George Withington on August 29, 1721, bargained with him. In return for a payment in cash of 13*s.* he was induced to sign a paper to find work and not be on the rates in future. His receipt and undertaking are printed in an appendix. As far as Atherton accounts show, the poor law was not in any sense grinding. Apprentices were indentured and not only was the fee paid but also the costs of the indentures and the stamping of them in London. The overseers even kept a stock of furniture, which included a pair of bedstocks and loaned them out to those in the eventide of life who were without roof, friends or means of sustenance. Connelly's wife in 1747 had from William Low utensils sufficient for her restricted needs. Once the bailiff had distrained upon a debtor and not finding enough to satisfy, took the man's working tools. It was a harsh thing to do. The overseers forthwith bought him a new set. If the lord's lease required the tenant to repair the house, in deserving cases the cost was borne by the overseers. It might be a new thatch or a wall needing daub and mortar, The old chapel did not escape their attention or bounty. In 1694 the overseers bought a desk for use in the meeting house and three years later they glazed all the windows, which were broken. Even when a preacher came they bore part of the cost of treating him. Mr. Sale came in 1707 and 1*s.* 3*d.* was spent on him. Poor women receiving either in-relief or out-relief were given gladen or welsh flannel to make shifts. Spinning wheels and iron for old nailors are included in many purchases which instance a high appreciation of the value of honest work.

## THE CONSTABLES OF ATHERTON, 1692

Township constables were important officers in their time and day. There were two; in growing centres, assistants could be appointed; and in Atherton there was a constable for the higher side and one for the lower. They were elected at the town's meeting and took office from October 20 for one year. The first duty was to get sworn before a local justice of the peace and this cost the ratepayers 6*d.* By comparison with the overseers of the poor, the amounts they disbursed were small. In 1694 they spent £3 11*s.* 3½*d.* It could so come about that the estimated expenditure exceeded the expenses and the outgoing constables paid over the money to the new officers. George Smith in 1695 owed the town £1 5*s.* 6½*d.* from his balances. Each year end of office the accounts were scrutinized and signed by some of the more substantial townsmen, some of whom had filled the office themselves. Their chief concern was to keep vagrants on the move and get them on their way before trouble could arise over the question of a settlement. Many items of expense were small sums given to this floating element of society. If a beggar was lame, the constable hired a horse; and in 1692 they took a poor cripple as far as Deane church to be certain thereby that he was well and truly out of Atherton. Women big with child were nightmares to the constables; a confinement could mean a liability on the rates for many years. Township constables worked under the eye of the superior officer, the high constable of the West Derby Hundred, who sent his precepts to the petty constables of each town to collect money for repairs to bridges, pay the salaries of the governor of the house of correction at Preston or Manchester, the costly upkeep of Lancaster Castle and the purchase and repair of workglooms and tools kept there for the prisoners to work with. One special liability of the petty constables was the good state of the stocks. Struggles to get the offenders inside often resulted in damage; in 1699 Rowland Houghton spent 3*s.* 6*d.* for new wood; in 1751 Lawrence Brownlow fixed an iron part, cost 1*s.* 4*d.*, and in 1796 a new set of stocks had to be provided. Another important officer who came into close association with the village constables was the coroner. Inquests were arranged for him in the chapel, when anyone had been found drowned or dying in the highway, as was Matthew Cowood, a nailor, at Chanters Bridge in 1751. The office of petty constable was unpopular, involving unpleasant duties, such as the pricking of the militia, especially in the times of the great wars of the 18th century. Here the obligation was to make a list of all suitable men for army service and then, blindfold, prick with a pin enough names to satisfy the captain sent down by the War Ministry to recruit his company strength. The constables, like the poor overseers, took under their especial eye the repairs of the Bent chapel. They expended public money on the bell, the bell wheel, ropes, grease, and paid for repairs to the slates on the roof. After all the chapel came in useful for so many different needs of a public nature.

## THE MARKET, 1693

A market existed at Atherton from early times. Fairs, unless of ancient prescriptive right, were the prerogative of the local lordship and stallage dues were paid to the manor lord. Atherton market grew up around the chapel and school soon after 1645. The site was convenient, located where busy cross-roads converged. References to this early market are rare, but about 1693 among the constables' accounts is a payment of 2*s.* 6*d.* "for going about ye towns business concerning ye clerk of ye Market". In 1699 the fish stones were put up in the market place, for constable Rowland Houghton paid for their carriage to Atherton. These stones were permanent features of local market places: pedlars displayed wares for sale on them, besides fresh fish.

## OBSTINATE RICHARD RATCLIFF, 1699

Each tenant in the township was liable to repair the main roads according to his proportionable assessment. The highways overseers gave due notice that on a certain day work would begin and if a cart was needed for loading, then one had to be provided. It could happen that the tenant of the holding might be a minor or a woman and in such cases a substitute had to be found and paid for. In 1699 the road surveyors were Henry Morris and Thomas Thropp. They had warned Ratcliff to report and bring a cart with him. He had refused and complaint was made to two justices of the peace, who caused Ratcliff to appear at a private sessions in Leigh and explain.

## MEDICAL CARE IN ATHERTON IN 1700

A great dog had bitten in an extraordinary manner the leg of a very old woman, Mary Mills. William Smith, a surgeon, took her in his care and effected a difficult cure. Her life would have been in danger if Smith had not taken an interest in her, but she had no money to pay him and he sent his bill for £3 to the overseers of the poor; they slighted his work and refused to pay. Smith then saw some influential men, Mr. Bradshaw, Ralph Egerton, Charles Manwaring, Thomas Gellybrand, Peter Holcroft and John Hindley, who sent a letter to Hugh, Lord Willoughby of Parham. The outcome was an order for the overseers to appear before two justices and explain why they had not paid.

## THORPS IN CHOWBENT, 1701

Thropps were of Norse descent and are found in all parts of the old parish of Leigh. Richard Thorp died in 1708 and was nailor. John Thorp was a farmer, whose distaff members of his household increased their slender exchequer by spinning. He died in 1701, and left his family £6 of bad debts out of a total of £76 7*s.* 4*d.* His widow Ann and Giles Marsh, fustian weaver, certified the true value of his stock and goods. He had four cows and a calf, one cow called (like so many on local farms) by the name of Brandock, another Broad, and one more descriptively Two Tales, as the widow wrote. Thorp's hat was more than usually cared for; it was kept in a case.

## GILES GREEN, 1701

He was a nailor, but in contrast to his townsmen of the same name and kin he was hardly well-to-do with £31 3*s.* 4*d.* Of this full total £10 was in debts described in the language of his day as "sperate or desperate", hopeful or bad. When he walked abroad on muddy lanes he donned gamashers. His bellows, polls, irons, anvil, head hammer, smithy board and chest were in the shop, and in the barn oats, hay and stoops of straw for his pack-horse. The heirloom book of Mr. Perkins he still treasured and read, evidence in his inventory that he descended from that worthiest of sturdy stock so loyal to Parson Wood.

## THE CONSTABLES OF ATHERTON, 1704

In the year previous John France and Peter Smith had been elected constables for Atherton township. At the end of their year of office they cast accounts, which showed in hand a sum of £3 6*s.* 2*d.* But this money the constables refused to hand over to the new officiants, who were obliged in January 1704 to apply to the bench of justices for a peremptory order demanding that the said sum be immediately paid over. Their petition is printed elsewhere.

## EARLY COLLIERS, 1706

Atherton over a long period of historic time has owed much of its wealth in large measure to its coalmines. During the early years of the 18th century official records begin to describe local townsmen by their calling and particular livelihood. In 1706 John Wadkinson in his petition for poor relief was described as collier; so was John Morris in 1715.

## LANCASHIRE CHEESE, 1715

Leigh and the surrounding townships were famous for the excellent quality of rich fat cheese and the fame of these products was known throughout the kingdom. William Twiss, a fustian weaver of Chowbent, asked in his will that Edward Marsh should buy 224 lb. of cheese and send it to his brother-in-law, Mr. Francis Woolen in London. For this purchase he set aside £3 out of his small assets of £16 16*s.* 4*d.* Twiss had a sister Jane and he ordered that she was to have all the clothes of his wife, should he die before her. Twiss carried his shrewdness further. Giles Marsh had paid no rent for some time for the house Twiss let him have. So Twiss left a press to John and a chest to Samuel, both sons of Giles, but they were not to have them until the father had settled up his rent.

## THE SALE OF A SMITHY, 1720

George Taylor, one of the long succession of nailors, had died. He was far from being affluent and his friends Thomas Hayhurst and Peter Collier reckoned his assets to be £13 6*s.* 4*d.* They approached John Green, a nailsmith, and offered him all the contents of the smithy, which he had agreed to take over for £4 15*s.* 4*d.* The purchase comprised the wheel bellows, stocks, weighs, stiddy and other materials.

## THE 1715

The rebellion of 1715 holds a special interest for Atherton. For Parson Wood of the Bent chapel assembled members of his congregation and marched north to Preston, where the Scots making for the Ribble crossings were intercepted. The general of the Hanoverian forces assigned to the stout Chowbenters the task of guarding the ford at Penwortham. Much of what happened in November of this year has passed into folklore and legend save for one certain fact; Parson Wood earned for himself the title of "General". On the irrefutable side of witness to this great event are the constables' accounts for the year, when James Hope and Robert Kearsley faced a very steep rise in expenses due to the rebellion. They were in office for that year and spent the large sum of £25 7*s.* On November 13 they laid out 1*s.* 6*d.* going to Preston with the militia; earlier they had purchased bills and a scabbard. George Chow's work on the weapons of the soldiers and the volunteers earned him 14*s.* 8*d.* and Henry Bolton 5*s.* When the Chowbent heroes brought back news of the victory at Preston the constables allowed coal for the bonfire. The largest single outlay was £6 11*s.* 8*d.* paid to five men of the king's army. Both constables found their year of office burdensome with these high political troubles. They had been obliged to go to both Wigan and Newton with baggage transport and on December 15 the cost of 15 saddle horses to take captured rebels to Warrington and Lancaster cost the ratepayers of Atherton £4. At Holliwells in Chowbent the wives and children of two soldiers were lodged for one night and the constables paid the charges. When two wounded soldiers appeared in the town after the engagement, gratitude and charity inspired the constables to give them 1*d.* each out of the rates. Items of expense continued to appear in the accounts of the succeeding year 1717.

## THE NEW BENT CHAPEL, APRIL 23, 1722

When Richard Atherton's steward turned the dissenters out from their small brick edifice, it became necessary to find other meeting space until the time the new chapel on Nathan Mort's land was ready. Roger Rigby on the day above wrote to the Quarter Sessions at Ormskirk and petitioned that his dwelling-house at Atherton might be licensed.

*"Gib Fold", Elizabeth Street, Atherton.*
*Sometime Chowbent Chapel Parsonage*

## CAR BANK, 1709

Carr in old place names meant a clearing and then a house was usually built. At Car Bank in 1709 died Ralph Leigh, who had added new buildings to his homestead. Several of his fields bore by their particular names evidence of these clearings, the Carrs and Mean Carrs. His range of buildings formed a fold, with a hedge useful for laying clothes on to dry after they had been washed. When Henry the eldest son took over, he had to raise £300 for John, Peter and Mary in order to bring into balance the expense of the new additions. Leigh left an average of £66 9*s*. 9*d*. and in his household was a spice box. When his sister Margaret died in 1702 Ralph was her "whole executor". These Leighs of Chowbent had some close association with Blackrod and Rivington. George Brownlow of Rivington was uncle of Mary Leigh, Margaret's sister and had left to her at some time Ward's Tenement.

## THE NEW ENGLAND COLONIST, 1722

John Marsh was the son of John Marsh and against his father's wish and without his consent he had emigrated to New England and to other remoter parts beyond the seas. On July 9, 1722, the father John altered his will and revoked a legacy of £150 to him and arranged for the money to go to four of his sons-in-law.

## OUR MASTER'S BIRTHDAY, 1722

Mad Richard Atherton's respect and esteem must have suffered in consequence of the ejectment from the chapel. It was a high-handed act of authority. When he married, the constables on February 17, 1718, spent 17*s.* on a bonfire and caused the ringers to peal the bell of the chapel in his honour. That was reasonable in 1718. But in 1722 things were different and the relationship of landlord, tenant and townsman had become strained. Nevertheless the constables paid 2*s.* 6*d.* for the bells of the Bent Chapel to be rung on May 21, 1722, in honour of his birthday. It was a strange act of deferential humility, when the bell had to ring out in respect of one who had turned the congregation out of house and were at the time actually worshipping in barns.

## THE VILLAGE BLACKSMITH, 1723

The horseshoe smithy of Richard Underwood was held on lease from Richard Atherton and when the blacksmith died in 1723 he passed on the unexpired term of the three lives to yeoman James Hope and nailor Robert Marsh; if these could not use up the time, then to the Hindley family. Underwood had only nephews as his near relatives and to three of these he left 5*s.* each. In his lifetime he had been a devout worshipper at the old Bent Chapel and remembering the joy of his community there in that small brick edifice of a meeting house, he gave 20*s.* to Mr. James Wood and a like gift to the Rev. Mr. John Wood of Horridge. The smithy where he used his tools and earned his livelihood was valued at £2. Debts due in Cheshire owed to his brother amounting to £8 had still not been paid to him. On the shelves in the house were several books, including the works of Isaac Amber. His bellows, priced at 5*s.* because they were old, was his only worktool which is listed. The total value of all he had was £41 16*s.* 7*d.* Among his many possessions rarely finding a mention in local records were six whesens. As they are bracketed with his various chairs, they were probably footstools.

## ATHERTON HALL, 1723

Mad Richard began the building of Atherton Hall in 1723. The foundation stone was laid and inscribed: "marcij 28 1723 Rics Atherton Ar W W: Ar. Archs". It was discovered at the demolition of the building a century later. The architect was William Wakefield. A full description of the Hall appeared in Colin Campbell's *Vitruvius Britannicus* published in 1725. When an Irish bishop, Richard Pococke, came to Leigh in 1750 he left the main road to see the building. He notes that it was not finished nor kept in good order. Ionic fluted pillars and pilasters supported the 102-feet-long façade.

## RICHARD ATHERTON, 1726

He was only 26 when he died. He is memorable for two events, which happened during his short life. He turned the congregation out of Chowbent chapel, that small brick edifice, and he began the building of a fine new residence for himself, Atherton Hall, a testimony to his pride, vanity and insanity. It was too grandiose. Building began in 1723, the rearing ceremony, when the whole was roofed, came on September 3, 1724, and the Hall completed in 1743. Nothing of this great pile remains to this day, which was to be the home of the Athertons to replace the moated Lodge. A fine tree-lined avenue led from the Hall portico to the church at Leigh and over a splendid ornamental bridge spanning an artificial stretch of water. This mad Richard married Elizabeth Farington, daughter of William Farington. A portrait of her dated 1726 still survives.

## THE GLASSHOUSE, 1727

The Glasshouse was a peculiar name affixed as a local landmark in the Atherton area adjacent to Leigh boundary. The highways surveyors bought "sleck" from the Glasshouse in 1733 and paid 5*s.* for ashes to spread upon the roads. William Farnworth in 1727, when he married at Leigh church, described himself as clerk to the Glasshouse. The once well-known name was in common use as late as 1893, when there were tanks associated with its location. The Tithe Map of 1839 gives the Glass House a marked prominence in its isolation.

## NO MONEY FOR HIS FUNERAL, 1727

A nailor, Robert Allred, had no money to pay for his burial expenses. Costs had been rising since Elizabethan days, when a twinter calf could be sold to defray these inescapable charges. So he asked John Collier, in the same trade as himself, and fustian weaver Henry Hayhurst to pay for the funeral and recover the outlay from the income of his tenement. His moveables in the house and smithy were totalled up to £42 5*s.* 0*d.* Robert the son inherited the house and smithy, paid £10 to his sister Margaret and brought up Alice till she was able to earn her own livelihood.

## THE MILLER OF ATHERTON, 1728

Millers Lane today still commemorates this vanished landmark of former social and economic times, the corn mill of the manor to which every tenant had to send his corn to be ground, unless excused or made hopper free. Usually millers died well to do, for society ascribed their gains to dishonesty and the wide difference between the weight of grain delivered in and what the miller bagged out for the customer. Thomas Tildesley was miller before 1728 and left less than £40. He lived while working the mill at Heys Tenement. Ellen was his wife, Ralph the eldest son and £20 was to be divided between his other children, Thomas, Elizabeth and Margaret. Judging from his signature he was old and shaky when he died.

## A GIFT OF COMMUNION PLATE, 1723

Samuel Hilton, chapman and merchant of Bedford donated the massive silver communion service to the episcopalian chapel, for when the Wood congregation was evicted they took with them their communion cups and an oak table. Hilton was one of the richest men of his time and a friend of George Ward, the vicar of Leigh. He died in 1727.

## A GREAT BIBLE IN THE NEW CHAPEL, 1728

Chowbenters sometimes kept books in their pews at the chapel; they could follow better the discourse of argument running as a thread through the sermon or verify the texts on which they were based by the preacher. Nailor Thomas Hayhurst let his great Bible lie in the chapel which he had helped to build. He gave to minister Wood the sum of 50*s.* and said if any family bequest lapsed, that too should go towards the stipend he received. A nephew, Richard Hayhurst, was given the Bible and the remainder of his £77 16*s.* 2*d.* was for four daughters, Mary, the eldest, and Martha described as the "midmost". Hayhurst as nailor worked the Rock smithy. A kinsman Henry Hayhurst busied himself with all his affairs and a letter (still preserved) was sent to him that he was to collect all the papers and documents at the White Bull in Warrington and so avoid the long trek to Chester.

## CHOWBENT CHAPEL SCHOOL, 1734

Among the deeds of this chapel is one dated January, 1, 1734, when John Mort conveyed to Ralph Astley and others the site of the parsonage and part of the school site. This land was taken from Alder Fold or as it was then described Owler Fold. The school was not the grammar school, where Edward Sedgwick was teaching. It was a separate building, erected by the evicted congregation soon after 1722 in order that the children of dissenters might be taught the true principles of religion away from the influence of the Episcopalian chapel. On the school site was a house for the master, a stable, back kitchen and garden. Many of the ministers taught in the school and the cottage came to be let, for in 1788 it was occupied by Cicely Valentine. On May 12 of that year the chapel trustees leased the school site and buildings to Peter Valentine at a yearly rent of 50*s.*

## THE ESTATE SURVEY OF 1734

This magnificent tome gives, as its title shows, a full survey of Atherton in this year. It is the most important record preserved among the Lilford muniments. It gives the name of each tenant and the size of his holding. Inevitable changes of tenancy have been pencilled in by a later hand. Flashes of entrancing detail are thrown across the local scene of 1734. Richard Robinson's cottage and smithy was in the same length as the school. Thomas Smith had house and garden "over against" the meeting house or the new chapel. Peter Collier lived at Chanters and Edward Laithwaite at Crabtree. Among the better-off tenants on the estate were Mr. Roger Rigby and Mr. Adam Mort.

## CHOWBENT CHAPEL FIELDS, 1734

In the great Book of Estate begun in this year for the better clarity and understanding of the manorial officers, there is an intriguing entry of certain fields named as the Park Ground, Four Acre, Seven Acre, Less Seven Acre, nearest Rylands Park, further Rylands Park, and great Rylands Park. The entry says "for the use of the chappell given by R. Atherton Esquire but without deed". Rylands Parks were well known and were situate near the Avenue. Which Richard gave these fields to the chapel—the Jacobite or the insane? Like the ground on which the first small brick edifice stood, no legal estate had been transferred.

## CHOWBENT CHAPEL PARSONAGE, 1735

In 1735 a new parsonage was built nearer to the chapel, where the ministers could now be located. This was the official residence of the chapel ministers to the date of the migration to Harrison Parsonage along Bolton Road. The old house became tenanted by the chapel caretaker.

## THE OLD CHAPEL OF CHOWBENT, 1741

Yeoman Thomas Garnett was the tenant of two houses in Chowbent; the one he lived in and the other was in the occupation of Ruth Sharples. In a very short will it was stated that if the son Thomas failed to continue the line, then his share in these houses was to be sold and the money given to the poor "who shall constantly come and attend morning and evening service at the old Chapel in Chowbent each Lord's Day to buy bread".

## CHURCH RATES, 1742

Atherton as one of the six townships of the old parish of Leigh from the earliest of times to the middle of the 19th century was obliged to pay towards the upkeep of the mother church. This rate like other assessments was levied on a compulsion basis and in course of years, with the growth of dissent, became unpopular. There were refusals from time to time and in 1742 Joseph Hatton would not pay, although his liability was only 2*d.* Congregations like those of the New Bent chapel and the Countess of Huntingdon chapel at Tyldesley objected to this rate, when for the fabric of their own chapels they had to rely upon gifts and bequests. The 1743 churchwardens' accounts show the Reverend James Wood paying his quota of 2*d.* towards the state church in Leigh. These were modest sums, but substantial hereditaments like Green Hall and Chanters paid 3*s.* 2*d.* and 3*s.* 8*d.* The total rate for Atherton in 1805 was £25 3*s.* 10*d.*, so that the entire parish paid six times that amount. Eventually the church rate became so great a source of trouble that it was quietly dropped. Expenses paid to the parish church covered many benefits which the outlying townships enjoyed, the upkeep of the burial grounds and the extension in 1828 with their right to share the charities. But repairs to the church, surplices, cost of bread and wine, visitation fees and ringing of bells and coals for heating were alien to those who never once came to the established church. Attempts to enforce the rate, Easter dues and tithes created bitter acrimony among quite loyal parishioners. The last time an attempt was made to levy a church rate in Leigh was in 1854.

## HAGFOLD, 1742

A branch of the Aldred family lived for a long time in Hagfold. Like the Withingtons, Rigbys, Marshes, Greens, Smiths, and Walkdens, they wove family history into the wider context of local events and lent a sense of stability to the social order of their day. Aldred meant in the Saxon tongue wise counsel and was as evocative of long and sturdy ancestry as was Shakeshaft. Mary Aldred widow died in the winter of 1742 and everything that she owned and treasured, even down to the mousetrap, was once noted for posterity to know. Among the very numerous items she kept in her Hagfold home was a nursing chair and a candlestick for a weaver. Her books included a volume of Mr. Boise, a Bible and a smaller one with clasps. John Hayhurst was her brother-in-law and at his Chowbent house there was belonging to her a pair of bedstocks, chaff bed, bolsters and blankets. Most of what Mary had cared for in her lifetime was given to Nicholas Withington. In 1751 another relative and widow, Mary Aldred, died and again Withington the nailmaster came to inherit. The daughters of this second Mary were Ann, Martha and Mary. In 1765 Robert Aldred died. There is not much to detail about him; he had an interest in Turtons and Sales Cottages; his wife was Sarah, James, a son, Sarah and Elizabeth, daughters, and a granddaughter Catherine. The book of Mr. Boise was a collection of sermons by the 17th century divine, Edward Boys. He was a friend of Bishop Hall and died in 1667. At a guinea the volume was high priced.

## PLATT FOLD, 1745

Platt Fold was to the year 1899 part of Atherton; when Leigh was incorporated as a borough, this area of Atherton was annexed to Leigh. That the lordship of Atherton extended right to the Avenue Gates with the mother church just across the highway is ample evidence of the might and worship of the Atherton family in former ages, establishing influence over church and market alongside the manors of Pennington and Westleigh. Platt Fold derives its name from the platt or fording over the brook and in its fold lived many generations of the Platt family. John Platt, a linen webster, on August 21, 1645, re-leased his home to John Atherton; it had been held by the father John Platt. The renewal fine was £13, yearly rent 10*s.* and the boons one day's shearing, a quarter-day loading dung, one and a half days harrowing with a double harrow, and one half-day with a single harrow.

## THE 1745

Constables for the township were John Baxter and John Morley. Compared with the 1715 their expenses were light. These were £5 16*s.* 8*d.* paid to the militia on October 13. When the rebels arrived at Leigh on October 28 they spent 2*s.* 6*d.* of town money and a like sum on October 28 for the journey to Manchester and horse hire "with the rebels". The constables of Pennington bore the heaviest expenses. In Atherton on the second rebellion there were no quarterings paid for and no repair to weapons or swords, which suggests the Scots did not halt in the town.

## ROAD WIDENING, 1747

Increased traffic betwixt Leigh and Bolton obliged the town surveyors of Atherton to buy roadside land and extend the width of the coseys. Robert Gwillym sold verge land to the town this year which cost £21 9*s.* 3*d.* In 1768 there was a further sale to the township of a value of £15 3*s.* 8*d.* And a part of the demesne land had to be bought to widen Stockplatt Lane near the church in Leigh. Platts were a common method of fording streams at this period; shallow approaches were constructed allowing easy passage through the water for carts and stepping stones for wayfarers. The town surveyors had constantly to look at these fordings in Bag Lane and at Green Hall to keep them in passable condition and clear of debris.

## CINDER HILL, 1756

Life in Atherton was growing socially more complex during the course of this and succeeding centuries. New livelihoods and occupations begin to be noted. William Aldred was an apothecary or chemist, who died in 1756. To his wife Elizabeth he left houses in Swinton, Monton and Atherton. In Chowbent he lived at Cinder Hill and he directed that the life of his niece, Martha Davenport, should be added to the lease. Aldred left no issue himself, but notes a cousin, William Aldred, son of Thomas, and uncle William Aldred of Pendleton.

## THE ESTATE MAP OF 1760

The map dates from about this year and gives the names of each field except the Alder Fold lands belonging to Ralph Astley. They are now a faint reminder of arcadian Atherton, a landscape transformed and scarred by industry. Today the survival of many place names with fold is a witness to the past ways of life of generations that toiled and laboured hard in these pleasant pastures. Fold denotes a range of buildings, where the tenant could bring his flocks and herds in winter and where he could store his crops. In early days the folds formed a square, homestead, barns and cottages for the workers, easily accessible to a supply of water. Gib fold is descriptive for gib meant a crook in the stream; Alder fold, Common fold, Bee fold are easily explained. Hag fold was the place where a stunted shrub grew, which was much used for hurdles and fences. Most street names are not historic; they acquired titles from the market towns to which they led, Leigh Road, Bolton Road, Wigan Road, while many of the modern streets are, except for a few, quite detached from any local origin. Mealhouse Lane harks back to its industrial epoch, when the working class of the mills and mines fed on oatmeal and milk as a diet to sustain their toil and sweat. Flapper Fold was the place where partridges took to the wing from their nesting place.

## THE FIRST FLETCHER, 1776

John Fletcher was very much alive to the great industrial possibilities of coal mining in these parts of Atherton and in 1776 began the sinking of two shafts under a lease granted to him and Thomas Guest by Robert Vernon Atherton Gwillym, who died in 1783. A reference to this lease is in a letter of July 25, 1821, when Hodgkinson, perusing the lease, wrote that Fletcher was forbidden to mine coal under the Hall, the Lodge or the Old Hall demesne. He had to keep his pits away from these local landmarks. In very early days much capital was needed to finance a venture like the sinking of a pit and Fletcher joined with Thomas, John and Christopher Guest of Bedford for help. Later differences inevitably arose and to compose matters Ralph Fletcher, the son of John, offered £800 to buy out the Guests' share in the Atherton coalpits. The lease was to run for 99 years from June 24, 1776. The terms provided for 1*s.* for every pit load of 30 baskets and each basket to contain 120 lb., payable to Gwillym and his successors, which was mined and sold at 2*d.* per basket and 1*s.* 6*d.* for every pit load sold at 3*d.* per basket.

The Hall, offices and gardens had coal and slack unlimited, but Lilford, when he sold out to Fletcher in 1821, agreed to take only each year 250 tons of such coal free for general use. Fletcher was bound annually to raise 2,000 pit loads, exclusive of the free coal. In the lease preserved among the Lilford deeds, Fletcher is described as of Tonge with Hough and Guest a yeoman of Bedford.

## "THOU SHALT NOT PREACH IN CHOWBENT CHAPEL", 1768

A very pious member of the nailor family of Withington was Richard, who died in 1768. He was well to do and left £500 in trust for his son Nicholas, who was a scholar at Stand school and there he was to remain till he was 14. A similar sum was left to a daughter. But of this large fortune from trade in nails, should the two young children not live till they were 21, then £200 of this sum was to be put to interest and the money paid to the meeting house at Chowbent, Samuel Mercer, minister there, being a trustee along with Withington's brother-in-law Richard Hatton, but only on condition that the Rev. William Davenport, minister at Hindley, be never allowed to preach in the pulpit or perform any part of the service there. Then he continued with bequests of £100 to the chapels at Wrightington, Darwen, Walmesley and Ashton-in-Makerfield, with a special gift to Samuel Mercer, minister at Chowbent, who along with Hatton was trustee for all these bequests. Richard Aldred, an innkeeper in Atherton, with these two were the executors appointed and nominated by this strange nailor of Atherton. Davenport was in Wood's later years his assistant and succeeded him as minister from 1759 to 1765, when he left for Hindley. He was M.A. of Glasgow and at one time kept a school for the children of dissenters. He died in 1791.

## THE CHAPEL CLERK, 1772

The office of chapel clerk was endowed with some importance. At Leigh it was the parish clerk, who dealt with a wide range of duties. The administration of both church and chapel fell to them. In all three places, Leigh, Atherton and Astley the office was much sought after. Edmund Brown was clerk at the old chapel in Atherton from October 25, 1772, to October 30, 1779. The salary of the parish clerk at Leigh in 1787 was £6 a year.

## ROADS, 1770

Growth of industry and population in Atherton caused a great change for the better in providing good roads. For centuries forced labour was the means of keeping the highways and byways in sufficient service for the limited use then demanded of them. Townsmen worked their statutory six days on the roads, brought their carts, loaded local sand and ashes from the smithies, and kept the highways in serviceable condition. About 1770 a new idea of road concept was introduced, the turnpikes. Such a road was made betwixt Bolton and Leigh; it was hard surfaced and people invested money with the commissioners of the local turnpike trusts and from the tolls paid by travellers came the pool of money to maintain the road in repair and pay interest on the loans. The right to farm a turnpike gate was often sold and a purchaser relieved the trust of the necessity to man a turnpike and instead collected himself or by a servant and risked making a profit over and above what he had estimated would be the receipts for a year or a lease of several years. There was a turnpike trust house at the Atherton boundary on Bolton Road. The Atherton surveyors' records show plainly how the old system proved inadequate for a growing town. Instead of elected surveyors a full-time officer was appointed and paid. James Brown in 1797 was one of the earliest full-time surveyors and Giles Watmough, who died in 1823, was his successor. About the period 1775–99 huge quantities of paving stones were purchased and laid down There are day books for the years 1791–1821 which give full data about work done on the roads in Atherton. And these separate books of each year are continued by a red book of highways for the long period 1842–63. Before this time a separate ley or rate was levied, not the old tax based on the length of each frontager to the highways, but assessed according to the value of each tenement. These assessments were written in what are called "composition books", which begin in 1768 and finish in 1796, with two later detached books for 1836–7. The rate in the pound was usually 10*d.* and after each annual meeting had agreed the amount, the rate was "warned" or called out in St. John's church with the valuation book exhibited at one of the local inns. Martha Aldred had the book at the Bear's Paw in one year. Turnpikes were the feature of the day until the coming of the railways. Greater intercommunication and public opposition finally put an end to the system. There were all kinds of problems. If a person had no land he tried to escape the liability for working or paying his composition. In 1769 George Kenyon of Kenyon Peel advised the surveyors of Atherton that any person over 18 and not 65, even if he had no land, was liable to be called upon to do work on the roads. Only apprentices and domestic servants were exempt. On September 7, 1775, there had been a town meeting between Robert Gwillym and the local surveyors and townspeople. It was amicably agreed that he, the lord of the manor, should repair the road from Kirkhall Lane to Langley Platt and thence to the Grange and so to the Tyldesley boundary, while the town surveyors agreed to see to the length from the Hillock to Langley Platt. Thomas Brideoak, the steward and agent, agreed for the lordship and James Clowes for the town and nine substantial tenants in support. In such ways friction was avoided for a time and the problems perennial in their nature could only be solved by the setting up of a local statutory board endowed with powers adequate enough to solve the new problems which new ways of life had produced.

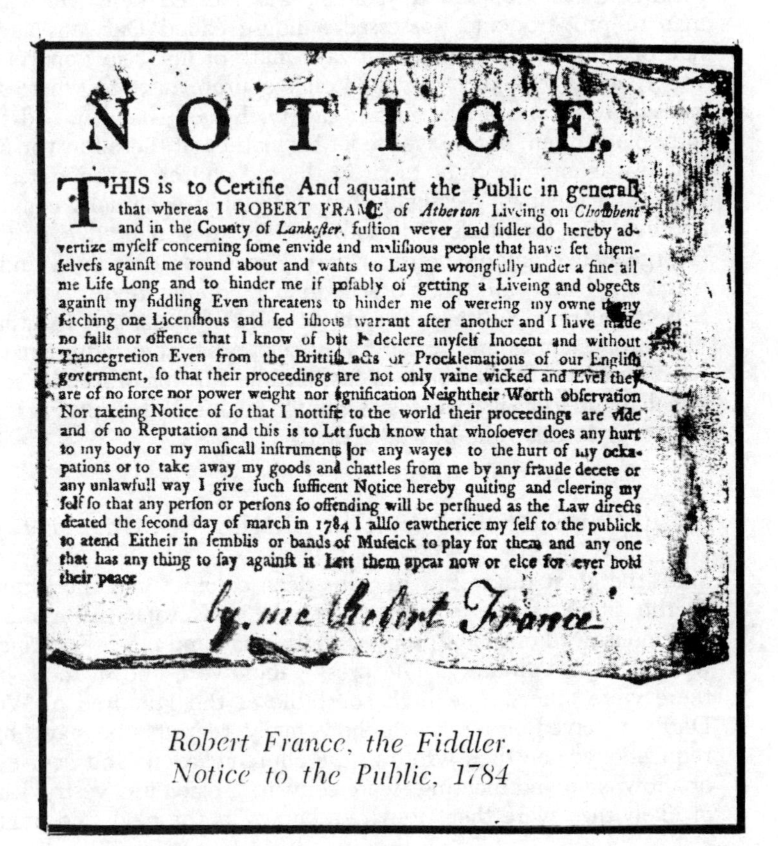

NOTICE.

THIS is to Certifie And aquaint the Public in generall that whereas I ROBERT FRANCE of *Atherton* Liveing on *Chowbent* and in the County of *Lankeſter*, fuſtion wever and ſidler do hereby advertize myſelf concerning ſome envide and maliſhous people that have ſet themſelveſs againſt me round about and wants to Lay me wrongfully under a fine all me Life Long and to hinder me if poſably of getting a Liveing and obgects againſt my fiddling Even threatens to hinder me of wereing my owne many fetching one Licenſhous and ſed iſhous warrant after another and I have made no fallt nor offence that I know of but I declere myſelf Inocent and without Trancegretion Even from the Brittiſh acts or Procklemations of our Engliſh government, ſo that their proceedings are not only vaine wicked and Evel they are of no force nor power weight nor ſignification Neightheir Worth obſervation Nor takeing Notice of ſo that I nottifie to the world their proceedings are vide and of no Reputation and this is to Let ſuch know that whoſoever does any hurt to my body or my muſicall inſtruments or any wayes to the hurt of my ockapations or to take away my goods and chattles from me by any fraude decete or any unlawfull way I give ſuch ſufficent Notice hereby quiting and cleering my ſelf ſo that any perſon or perſons ſo offending will be perſhued as the Law directs deated the ſecond day of march in 1784 I allſo eawtherice my ſelf to the publick to atend Eitheir in ſemblis or bands of Muſeick to play for them and any one that has any thing to ſay againſt it Lett them apear now or elce for ever hold their peace

by me Robert France

*Robert France, the Fiddler.*
*Notice to the Public, 1784*

## THE SPINNING JENNY WHEEL, 1777

When tremendous changes through inventions were taking place in the cotton industry, Mary Higginson, stepdaughter of James Scholfield, was still spinning on her jenny in 1777 in that ancient home of the Scholfields in far Atherton. John Scholfield followed his father James in this year with an uncle Edmund and aunts Betty, Anna, Ellen and Margaret given tenuous rights of succession.

## PLATT FOLD, 1777

John Brideoak, self-styled yeoman, was located here. He was a man of property and possessed a house called Darwells and a half of Robinsons. Another outward mark of his local importance was that he owned a pew in Leigh church, next to where the sidesmen sat, and a seat in the gallery. Robert, his son, had this lofty place room, but he was to let his mother sit there for worship. There was another right to sit in the old church appropriated to Parrs Tenement in Westleigh, but this would eventually come to another son, Jonathan. Brideoak's widow was offered a part of George Penkethman's house, where James Ranicars lived and it was hoped he would not object to her coming there, paying a reasonable rent. Substantial sums of £440 for the son Jonathan, £550 for Thomas and £250 for Robert, other sons, additional to what had been given them in his lifetime further prove the solid social foundation of Brideoak's family in this 18th century. Platt Fold was at this time part of Atherton.

## RECRUITMENT FOR THE ARMED FORCES, 1779

With the great quarrel of the American colonies and the coming of the titanic struggle against France in Europe, Britain had enormous need of men to serve in both army and navy. Enlistment was far from voluntary. The press gangs were one method, but there were others. The high constable of the Hundred of West Derby received orders as to how many recruits the navy had requisitioned; he then wrote to the churchwardens and overseers of a township and meetings were convened, often in a vestry. Lists of likely men were then prepared, known as the navy and militia ballot, and the names pricked. Those elected had to serve or find a substitute to stand in. On March 26, 1795, Atherton and Dalton had to send three men to serve afloat. The business cost the ratepayers dear, £54, for all expenses incurred at Liverpool and Prescot. Edward Jones, apothecary of Atherton, first examined them and found them fit in health. The next step was to send them to Liverpool to the regulating Captain of the Port of Liverpool, who certified their fitness for active service. Each recruit who passed the test received a generous bounty of £23. Recruitment for the army was much the same. Township officials took note of the army directions and prepared their lists. Among the Atherton town chest papers is an undated list of 165 subscribers of men of Chowbent eligible for military service. It contains the name of Giles Watmough, who was dater to become a paid surveyor and this would date the record about the end of the 18th century. Each man paid 1*s.* and the sum raised was to cushion the hardship caused by military service when a man had been chosen. A shorter second list states the money could be used to buy a stand-in. From 1779 a succession of Chowbent men acted as substitutes for men of the Derby militia. Facts about these men come from the accounts of the overseers of the poor, who paid out relief to the dependants of the men. Isaac Hurst served for William Hadfield of Hope in Derbyshire. By order of July 10, 1779, Atherton paid out relief of 3*s.* per week. Henry Caldwell, weaver of Atherton, served in the army for Samuel Cousins of Chesterfield, William Hatton for John Bagshaw of Abney, and Thomas Hatton for William Malburn. In 1782 Thomas Hatton was substituted for William Beeland of All Saints Parish in Derby, while John Jameson served for Jacob Hardey of Darley. Dependants of all these soldiers were in receipt of weekly payments from the overseers of Atherton during the period of the great imperial wars. One, John Seddon of Chowbent, was a member of the recruiting party of the 1st Regiment of Foot Guards about the year 1787.

## THE MILLER, 1792

Peter Aldred was miller of Atherton, working two mills, the old Hall mill and the Lodge mill, which Atherton Legh Atherton had leased to him. He left these with a property called Park Lane to his son John with the right of his mother to live there. A daughter Betty received a payment of £60 at 21. One half-year's rent of the two mills was £18 17*s.* 6*d.*

## THE OBELISK, 1781

Robert Gwillym erected the obelisk in Leigh market place in 1761. His son Robert Vernon Atherton decided in emulation that he would build a similar monument in the centre of Atherton's busy roads facing the present parish church. The cost then in 1781 was £32 16*s.* 6*d.* It was completely rebuilt in 1867 and renovated in 1960. John Anderton was the mason in 1781 and William Tomlin in 1867. Anderton, who died in 1802, when the value of his estate was under £300, left no issue. His wife was Alice and two brothers, Richard and Daniel.

## THE INITIALS IN THE GALLERY PEW, 1782

Parson Wood galleried his square meeting house and with horse-box pews designed it to seat 1,000. Before the installation of the organ rows of pews faced inward and not towards the preaching pulpit; these were reserved for the singers. In two of the pews sat once Caleb Wright, the Gladstonian Liberal M.P., and Charles Eckersley, the cotton magnate. Today their past association fills the place with that elusive fragrance of great achievement. The family pews gave an added intensity of individual worship to the corporate devotion of the whole community and on one of these pews on April 4 in the gallery I.C. carved his initials.

## AN INNKEEPER IN PRISON, 1783

William Fildes kept an inn in Atherton; financially it made him to fall into debt. Creditors—John Birchall of Rainford, maltster, Joseph Broster of Liverpool, wine merchant, and Benjamin Bancroft of Bolton—caused him to be seized for debt and sent to Lancaster castle. Fildes possessed some interest in Crab Brow cottage, occupied by nailor Robert Woodward, with 8 acres of land, 3 cottages tenanted by James Alred, Ann Radcliff, widow and cordwainer John Newton. The lease had not run out, but Fildes had mortgaged them for £250 to nailor Joseph Worthington. He was out of prison by 1786, for on January 5 of that year a grand concert of Handel's music was performed at his house, the sign of the King's Head, for the benefit of the singers at the New Chapel. From a footnote, advertising where tickets at 1*s.* 6*d.* could be bought, the names of the sellers in Chowbent reveal that it was Chowbent Chapel for the benefit of which the concert was given.

## A MAP OF LANCASHIRE, 1784

William Yates's map of the county enshrines for us today the rural aspects of the landscape around Chowbent, for the two parks of the Hultons and the Athertons dominate the whole scene, proclaiming the power of the great landowners of that day. The game of squire Hulton made many of the fields adjoining the park fence quite a loss to both Atherton and his tenants, for the deer, hares and rabbits nibbled off the crops and this followed through, in that there was no tithe that could be taken. Yates shows the built-up area of Bag Lane, the tenements around the chapel, but the most noteworthy feature are the many busy brooks coming from the higher land of Westhoughton and Tyldesley Banks to feed the Glaze. Early settlers of the Saxon race with an eye to such topographic contours called the place "the town of the little brooks".

## THE FIDDLER, 1784

Robert France was the fiddler of Chowbent; but besides this jovial calling, he earned a more reliable living as fustian weaver. He made a will 1781, which was not proved till 1804, when it was marked as of a value under £5. In the earlier year he had owned four cottages known as the Nook, three occupied by nailor John Atkinson, daughter Ann France, Henry Kerfoot, and the fourth he left to a half-sister, Mary Withington. His family included two sons Robert and Richard and one other daughter Catherine. In 1784 this fiddler published a printed notice warning his enemies who had maliciously set themselves against him conspiring to do him harm. As a priceless example of the purest Chowbent vernacular it has been illustrated herein, for by commendable care it has been preserved for posterity. Signatures on both will and notice tally in a remarkable degree in both form and flourish. In modern days Robert France would have availed himself of the "To whom it may concern" columns of the local newspapers.

## AN ATHERTON FAMILY SERVANT, 1786

Among the many servants the Atherton family must have engaged there stands out one George Garnett, about whom more is known. He died in 1786 and in spite of his poor wage as domestic servant he was well off at £300. He had lent £30 to a brother-in-law, John Thomason of Burnage, and with no hope of ever being paid he released this to him. Robert Ryding, steward to Richard Atherton at this date, was asked to invest one-third of the money for the profit of his sister Sarah Thomason. The faithful gardener William Slow witnessed the will. Another brother, who took another one-third of the money, was William Garnett.

## DORNING RASBOTHAM'S DESCRIPTION OF CHOWBENT, 1787

Rasbotham was a descriptive travel writer who wrote these words about Chowbent in 1787:

> "Several families have acquired fortunes by making spinning jennies and carding machines which they send into Scotland, Ireland and different parts of the kingdom. Some of the mechanics do not keep less than 30 journeymen employed in the business."

His description recreates those individual hives of industry where the master was busily employed with his day piece men and apprentices all striving in earnest application to make these new machines. Thomas Highs of Pennington had invented his jenny about 1771. Nail smithies had for centuries channelled the ingenuity of stout Chowbenters and this adaptability was now invading the cotton industry. Soon it found suitable outlet in nuts and bolts and in the coalmines. A century later Edward Ormerod invented a safety detaching hook to avoid overwinding of the headgear wheels and thereby saved many lives and accidents. That same engineering skill has persisted and is evident today in units such as Staveleys and Greenhalghs.

## ROAD REPAIRS, 1783

The legal duty to work on the roads was still enforceable as late as this year. Brian Arrowsmith refused to work the statutory three days and was fined 9*s*. But constable John Collier could find no goods to cover the distress he went to make and in view of his refusal he was sent for 3 months to the House of Correction. In 1791 the whole township was indicted at Quarter Sessions for neglecting a length of 872 yards of highway leading from Four Lane Ends to Leigh. Two substantial men of the town had to travel to Ormskirk and provide surety that the work would be done.

## ATHERTON HALL IN 1789

The costly residence was finished in 1742 and was at its best under the Gwillyms. When young Atherton Legh died, there followed the usual appraisal of effects and moveables to scale the fee payable to the diocesan consistory. Household furniture, linen, china, glass and other items were set down at £1,551 14*s*. 1*d*., the silver plate at £422, books at the surprising estimate of £409 9*s*. 0*d*., the family portraits, many of which found their way to America, at £383, but which are now fabulously priced, jewels at £253 6*s*., making a full total with horses, cows, sheep and implements at £402 14*s*., a grand composite sum of £3,336 3*s*. 1*d*. His father Robert Vernon, by will, had ruled that all, apart from the livestock, should remain at the Hall. Outside were woodlands famed for their landscape beauty. Long after the Hall had been demolished Squire Hulton asked Lord Lilford for some dog-roses from the Atherton woods to adorn his home. Deer grazed in the park fields, and along heated walls grew plum and peach trees. There was a bowling green, guns in the armoury, current newspapers on the tables. Many types of clock ticked in the silence of the vast rooms, which blind John Houghton wound up at an annual payment of 11*s*. Around the paved yard roamed dogs, one called Charles, and all fed on milk and oats, and a black-faced Galloway horse had strayed as far away as Winwick. There was a brewing chamber fragant with Worcester hops and twenty-two chimneys regularly swept by a woman, Eleanor Priest. Horses were given bran and the deer had beans. William Slow was the gardener, able to call for additional labour at heavy times. All molehills in the fields were regularly levelled and the woodlands guttered to get the water away. An imperious housekeeper saw to the smooth running of the great house for her master with the help of two maids and four menservants, not counting the gamekeeper.

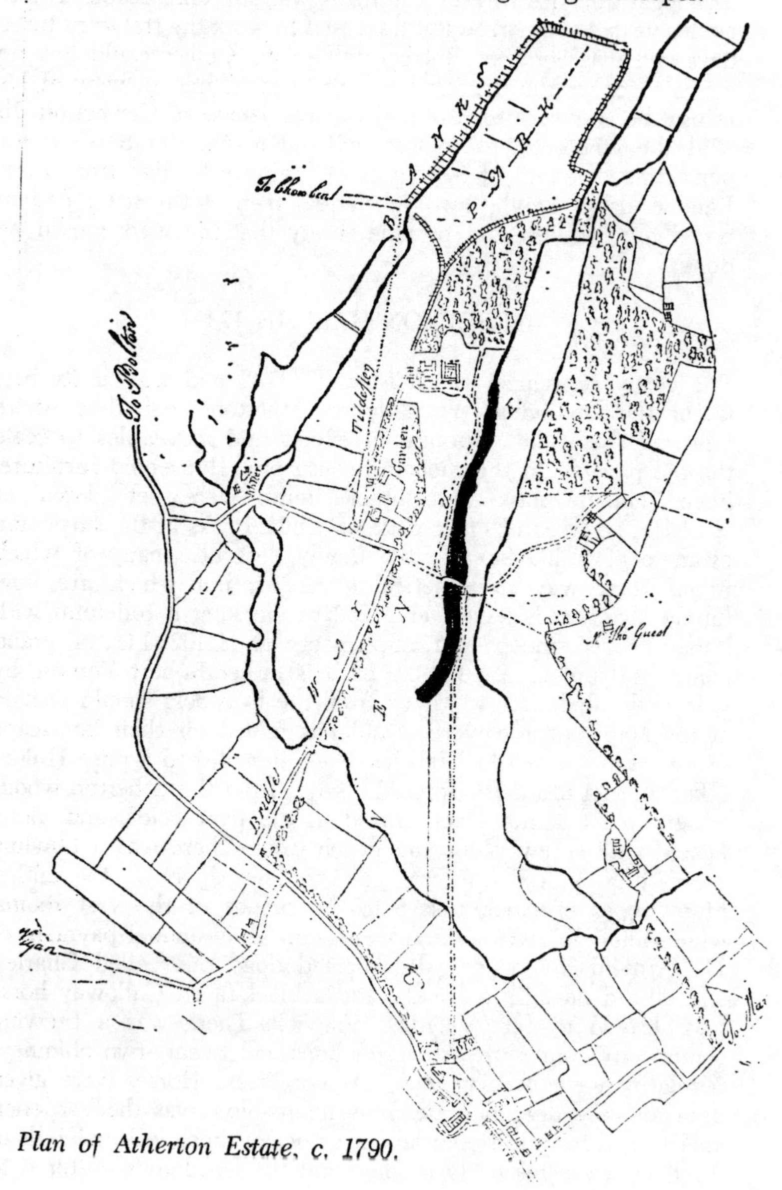


*Plan of Atherton Estate, c. 1790.*

## JOHN MORT, 1788

Mort belonged to that family of solid Presbyterians of the finest tradition, a name festooned with great distinction. He lived at Alder Fold with its eight cottages called Pendleburys and which he left by will to his friend Peter Valentine. A lease of Gibfold with some years yet to run he directed should be for the benefit of Chowbent chapel minister Samuel Mercer. Mort had no issue; John Rigby of Manchester was a nephew who took over a lease of Ringley Fold in Outwood. His personal estate came to £1,000. Other relatives he had were grandnieces Sarah Parry and Elizabeth Bunny. His sound friendship with Mercer inspired a gift of £20 additional to the lease. In 1791 Valentine acquired the small tithes of wool, pigs and lambs on Pendleburys from Simon Smith, a spindle maker of Tyldesley. Smith could deduce his title from a deed of October 11, 1700, when his great grandfather acquired them from Richard Eaton of Westleigh, whose family had inherited from the Urmstons.

## A JUST AND FAITHFUL STEWARD, 1791

Richard Hodgkinson was one of the most conscientious of that long line of stewards of the Atherton estates. He was son of Joseph Hodgkinson, who came from Horwich to live in Chowbent, and who, self-taught, became an itinerant writing master, visiting local schools. In 1771 Richard Vernon Atherton Gwillym and William Atherton Gwillym along with other trustees appointed him master of Leigh Free School. Here he stayed twenty years and in 1791 was succeeded by his son Richard, who had been master of the school at Chowbent since 1784. Both father and son were skilled in land surveying and estate management, for Joseph had worked for the great Duke of Bridgewater. Young Richard gained the confidence of the family of Atherton and was persuaded to give up the mastership of the school in 1791 and become their estates steward. In this employment he improved the financial condition of the Athertons immensely during the forty-five years he was their land agent. A fair number of records survive about him, for he was a great and prolific writer of everything that he did. From his account book and correspondence can be seen the policies and methods he pursued to win elusive prosperity for his master, himself and the tenants in an era of war and inflation.

## SWEARING IN A CHURCHWARDEN, 1792

The ancient offices of the township occasioned, besides personal inconvenience, much expense upon the elected representative. Sometimes these were met from the different rates. When a churchwarden was chosen, before he could act it was necessary to go to Chester, the then diocesan capital, and be sworn in. There office fees for Richard Clowes were 5*s;* swearing-in cost 6*s*. 8*d*., horse hire 12*s*. 1*d*., and a letter to Chester was 5*d*. Clowes then passed these on to the vicar of Leigh, Birkett, who saw the payment met from the church rate.

## CHOWBENT IN 1792

A very old fragmented directory of the inhabitants of Chowbent about this year has survived and is kept in Warrington library. It discloses the existence of many of the old inns. The village community was in the main dependent on farming and only two nailors, James Collier and Richard Manley, find a mention in the lists. Beyond this there is little trace of that industrialization which in the wake of a novel revolution was to overtake the town and transform its landscape, wealth and population. Thomas Hesketh was the sole manufacturer.

## BEAR'S PAW INN, 1792

This ancient hostel, now no longer existent, was kept by John Richardson in this year. It stood in a cluster of inns near to the chapel and offered its hospitality to the travellers on the turnpike roads. Often official business of the vestry was conducted in its rooms. Thomas Watson was at the inn in 1869 and later, in 1895, John Warburton. In close proximity was the Red Lion and the Queen's Head, on whose site was built the Westminster Bank. In 1866 Bear's Paw inn was rebuilt and possessed its own malt house. Thomas Warburton was then owner. Besides agenda of an ecclesiastical flavour, the town's annual meetings were convened there. A namesake, John Warburton, had the Queen's Head for a long period prior to his death in 1889. His tenants in 1869 and 1895 were Giles Higson and Joseph Edge. This now-vanished inn finds an early reference to its existence in 1838.

## STEWARD HODGKINSON ADVISES THE SALE OF THE HEREFORD ESTATES, 1794

When Robert Gwillym married Elizabeth Atherton he brought into settlement his estates in the counties of Hereford, Gloucester and Monmouth. Hodgkinson, when he assumed office as Miss Atherton's agent, found these properties greatly in debt and there was no prospect of improving them by way of increased rents. The only way to shed the liability was to sell them and he found he could do this under a private Act of Parliament which had been promoted by the Gwillyms about 1745. Both Mr. Rawsthorne and the young ward agreed with his plan and for two years he was engaged in the sale of these distant estates. With the money he received he paid off some of the charges on the Atherton settled lands and by this means he was soon in a position to take full advantage of his improved finances to set about increasing the income of the house of Atherton.

## THE END OF CHOWBENT GRAMMAR SCHOOL, 1794

Richard Hodgkinson was one of the last masters of this ancient school. He was nominated in 1784 and resigned in 1791 to follow his father as master of Leigh Grammar School. What Chowbent was like in numbers, financial prosperity and vigour can only be surmised, but Hodgkinson was a very capable individual. Notwithstanding, after his departure the life of the school after years of great service came to an abrupt and silent end. A letter of steward Hodgkinson in 1834 says he went to a select vestry in the old school near the King's Head. This was most likely the grammar school.

## A DISPUTE OVER TITHES, 1794

The destruction of the mansion house of the Lodge brought about in time difficulties over the payment of tithes. The Lodge, that moated seat of the early Athertons, enjoyed all the privileges of a capital house, capital meaning held direct from the feudal lord and tenant-in-chief at Warrington. Its demesne land was free from tithes. Before 1794 the Lodge was taken down by Peter Aldred's father and nearer to Chowbent, along Millers Lane, he built out of the materials another farmhouse to which the estate steward assigned 15 acres of the demesne land of the Lodge. The small tithes of Atherton had been bought by Mr. Clifton who sent his collector, Lawrence Heaton, for payment. Aldred paid under protest. Adam Howcroft, the tenant in 1794, refused to pay and the vigilant Hodgkinson supported him. Other parts of Lodge land had been put to Bee Fold, but had never been adjudged liable to tithes. The case came before the justices at Warrington, who ruled that demesne land, even if let out, was still exempt.

## THE ATHERTON ESTATES IN 1796

Young Richard Hodgkinson became steward in 1791 and his estate book which has entries in the year 1796 shows him to be busily occupied in the service of his mistress. This small paper volume continues its entries to the year 1802. The Powys were about this year improving Bewsey Hall and materials including deal planks, sashes and wet plaster hair were sent there from Atherton. A Chowbent carpenter and blacksmith from the estate were working on the hall. Hodgkinson paid all bills and managed the timber yard for Miss Atherton. He bought Worsley lime to repair his own house at Four Lane Ends and whenever possible he made profitable bargains to invest the surplus monies of the estate income. Richard Partington's buildings at Bridge Foot, part of the Bent End estate, had been taken by John Young. A new weaver's shop would cost £30 and repairs to the house £20. The steward made this bargain with him: bear the cost of timber for the repairs, pay a fine of £5 and the name of the wife would be inserted in the lease. Hodgkinson knew that because of the French wars timber would be scarce and dear. On the estate at this time was a brickyard near the Old Hall Mill. New Hall was sometimes occupied and the steward had to see to its provisioning with mutton, pork, wine and good old casks of ale. But Bewsey was the more favoured residence. There was a tenant at the Lodge and in 1798 seven sycamore trees growing in the orchard there he sold for £12 12*s*. Along the avenue a half-acre of grass was bought for £4 10*s*. in 1797.

Prices and rents were rising appreciably on the entire estate and two crofts at Leigh Gates were rented for £4. At Stock Platt he asked 8 guineas an acre for the land. There was a profitable brick kiln on the premises with bricks fired and burnt out of Hillock clay. Vermin did not escape the attention of the diligent and trusty steward and the address of Thomas Ormerod, rat-catcher of Langho Chapel was duly noted. There was good relationship between the lord, the steward and the tenantry, and Hodgkinson was told to pay a subscription of 10*s.* 6*d.* a year to each friendly and sick society in Atherton. In a bargain if the one party stood to lose, there was an instruction once given to be generous. John Unsworth in 1799 agreed to supply bricks for the use of the estate at 11*d.* per 1,000, but if he could not pay his labourers 2*s.* per day, the steward was to pay 1*s.* the thousand. Wigan tanners were buyers of bark. Hodgkinson sold oak bark at 6 guineas a ton, but the purchasers had to peel. And during a winter storm in 1802 five were uprooted and this windfall realized £35 for the estate. So well did young Hodgkinson manage the affairs of his absent master that Mr. Powys in 1799 increased his salary from £90 to £105 and back-dated it to June 24 of the previous year. The fortunes of the Athertons and their estates were bounding up in wartime to great heights of prosperity.

## THE OAK IN THE VALLEY, 1796

On the edge of the Valley watercourse grew an old oak. Mr. Valentine claimed it and cut it down. The ever vigilant Hodgkinson said it belonged to Miss Atherton and sold it to a timber merchant of Bolton. The steward watched his woodland; it was so valuable and he was keen on tree sales. He could get in the market 21*d.* per foot for sycamore. The local mines consumed a great amount of wood, oak being much in demand for ladders and pins in the underground workings.

## THE MARRIAGE SETTLEMENT OF 1797

Henrietta Maria Atherton upon her marriage with Thomas Powys brought into settlement all her lands and property rights. The draft extends to 69 double folio pages, which detail the manors of Atherton, Pennington, Bewsey, Burtonwood, Little and Great Sankey, Penketh, one-fourth of Westleigh lordship with the Old and New Halls of Atherton, Lodge, Bewsey Hall and Little Sankey Hall. Besides these extensive palatine lordships, there was income from Dallum, Warrington, Westhoughton and Woolston. The profits from Sankey Brook canal, one of the earliest examples of water transport in the country, the Fiddler's Ferry at Penketh and certain fisheries in the river Mersey were hers too. And add to these the prestige privileges of the advowsons of Warrington, Leigh and St. John's at Atherton, with the right to appoint a master for the Boteler school at Warrington, it must be conceded that Miss Atherton's fortune was very considerable. But there were profits from the courts, the mill tolls, kilns, royalties, tithes, frankpledge and all chattels of felons and fugitives. The settlement trustees appointed were Lord Grey of Wilton and Richard Gwillym.

## THE FIRST LORD LILFORD, 1797

Thomas Powys, the eldest son of his namesake father, was made a peer by Pitt in 1797. He assumed the title of Baron Lilford from his Northamptonshire estates. Under James II his great-grandfather had been attorney-general and in this office had prosecuted the Seven Bishops. As a Jacobite, the revolution of 1688 put an end to his political career. He retired from public life and purchased estates in Northamptonshire. Thomas Powys was given his peerage for political services. He was High Sheriff of Northants 1768–9 and M.P. 1774–97. As a youth he had been sent to Eton and King's, Cambridge. The letters patent creating him Baron of Lilford were sealed October 27, 1797. He died January 26, 1800, at the age of 56.

## THE BATTLE OF THE NILE, 1798

Nelson destroyed Napoleon's dream of power in the Middle East by this daring naval encounter. Richard Hodgkinson's own nephew John was serving in the navy and on his discharge settled in Gosport as a waterman. When news of the victory of Alexandria reached Atherton, Hodgkinson caused every house in the township to be illuminated in celebration.

## COAL PITS IN ATHERTON, 1800

There were many small pits winding coal about this year. From a colliery auditor's management book, which has survived, can be built up a picture in full detail of what conditions were in the industry. These pits were often in small local clusters and one was a drift pit, where the day's eye was constantly blocked by debris and had periodically to be cleaned up. The colliers were few in number, varying from 10 to 25 and for a day's work in November 1817 they earned 2*s.* 7*d.* Most of the pits had names to identify them, Old Engine Pit, New Engine Pit, where a gin driver worked, the Marsh Pit, Little Pit, Sough Pit and Crabtree Pit. One of the biggest items of expenditure was gunpowder; in 1801 as high as £13 4*s.* One concern of the management was with farming, to grow oats and wheat for the horses. To clean the coal the men used riddles. Much timber had to be bought and props cost 6*d.* each. Every so far pillars were left to support the tunnels. Tubs ran on rails fastened to sleepers by Chowbent nails. Taylor's foundry supplied in one year 646½ yards of iron rails. Candles lit the underground workings and to stamp out firedamp the men used a damper. As the coal was wound in baskets to the surface from the shaft pits two drivers, John Bowden and John Yates, loaded it to deliver to customers. Landowners got their quota of coal free, the word trust in the accounts coming before the name as "trust Lord Lilford". One woman, called Speakman's wife, earned 1*s.* 4*d.* a day for 4½ days in 1815. Colliers had free ale at Israel's and in their sickness the management bought wine for them. Not every week was a profit made; when there was a loss the auditor wrote "short" and when a profit "over". Regular burners of Atherton coal were Thomas Johnson of Tyldesley and Mrs. Froggatt of Astley, both extensive landowners. A side employment was the firing of bricks and many taxes such as brick duty, land tax and horse duty appear frequently in the expenses. Many of the appropriated trade words such as slack for fine coal, brows for the surface areas, and shunts for tubs, constantly illuminate this auditor's book.

## PETERLOO, 1819

Ralph Fletcher, colonel in the Yeomanry, was opposed to the radicals of south Lancashire. He was known among the working classes as the arch-fiend. Placed in the commission of the peace for Bolton division he was present as a magistrate in Manchester on August 16, 1819, when William Hulton, the chairman of the justices, gave the fatal order for the military to charge and the result was the massacre of eleven innocent victims. Hulton, Fletcher and another local justice, Richard Marsh of Westleigh, had signed an order declaring the meeting illegal. There had been large assemblies of demonstrators in Leigh and the question of law, order and protection of property had become most pressing in these parts of south Lancashire. Fletcher died in 1832. In his lifetime he was a martyr to lumbago.

## VISITORS AT PLATT FOLD, 1821

When Richard Hodgkinson became steward to Miss Atherton in 1792, he was then master of Leigh Free School and with that tact and caution which was his great virtue, he asked the feoffees if he could put in a deputy, James Blundel, and should he not be capable in his new duties he would be able to resume his former post. Hodgkinson stayed steward with the Athertons for 45 successive years; he remained friends all his life with Blundel. But this partnership was at times marred by friction. Blundel lived in Windy Mill Lane, the present Bradshawgate, and left Leigh for Crowland Abbey in 1808. He had studied for orders and had married, while at Leigh, a daughter of Mrs. Radcliff. She was at variant odds with Blundel and by her will left all her estate to the wife and nominated Hodgkinson executor to safeguard the interests of her daughter as sole beneficiary. This angered the clerical husband, who was very excitable, and in 1821 Hodgkinson invited them to come to Platt Fold to compose their differences. It was agreed that Hodgkinson should give up the management of the personalty, but keep that over the freeholds, an arrangement which brought £400 benefit to the husband. Blundel was at Crowland to his death, March 24, 1834; in 1810 he was instituted to the living of Waplode and the two combined incomes brought him £800 a year. Hodgkinson visited him in August 1822, when he was struck by the high standard of his domestic life, with a governess paid 30 guineas a year to teach his three daughters. Thomas Blundel, son of his reverend father, studied medicine and became President of the Royal Medical Society at Edinburgh. Hodgkinson for many years acted as agent for Blundel's properties in Leigh, which he reported in 1831 as very much sunk in value.

## ATHERTON COLLIERY IN 1821

On June 23 the auditor made a full account of all stock and assets of the 16 pits, which formed the group known as Atherton colliery. The total capital employed was £6,297 5*s.* 7*d.* compared with £8,005 14*s.* 7*d.* in 1819. The pit in Parson Horrocks's field was worked out and apart from 2,000 bricks there was not much to return at Hillock Pit. At the shafts known as Old Engine Pit, Engine Pit on Cox's farm and New Engine Pit the power was derived from waterwheels. At Further Atherton Engine Pit there were charcoal ovens valued at £50 with a rake hook and cross bars. There was little coal stacked except on Cox's Engine Pit. The various items of machinery included head gear, ropes, pulleys, capstans, gins, pump rods, banking hooks, pump trees, wagons, weighs, rails, damp grates and a counting house at Staith with its desk. At some pits there was a sharpening cote and grindlestones.

## JOSEPH WITHINGTON, 1822

Details about him and his possessions make him quite a character apart from his contemporaries. For he was well-to-do and had invested money in the Bolton-Westhoughton Turnpike and the Bolton-Leigh Turnpike. These road trusts were popular as offering a sound return on money invested in them and were not so speculative as loans in industry or to individuals. Withington specifies two sums with the Bolton-Leigh Turnpike, £330 and £160. He owned Knight's Farm, where Giles Watmough, one of the early paid surveyors of the town, lived. He died in 1822. Whitelees which Withington had let as tenant to Richard Aldred and Unsworth's and Warmingham's were his property. For investment, as cottage rents were becoming generally favoured, Withington had bought Dinah's Cottages and Sutton's Cottages. Further afield in Blackrod he owned Doodson's, which he disposed of to his son Peter. All told he was, apart from freeholds, worth £2,000.

## ATHERTON HALL, 1822

Between landlord and tenants in Atherton there had always been shown marks of mutual respect. The eviction from the chapel was one exception. The manor lord's birthday was made known to all by a peal of bells rung from Leigh church steeple; the birth or marriage of an heir was often celebrated in the town by a bonfire and ale at the town's expense. This traditional esteem harking back to those early times when the Athertons were always right worshipful and right honourable was a quality of social local life which was then seen as something to be perpetuated. On November 26, 1822, a great dinner was given at Atherton Hall on the occasion of the 21st birthday of the heir of Lord Lilford. Richard Hodgkinson sent out the invitation cards to local notables and estate tenants. Two years later the noble mansion was no more. On April 20, 1858, there were high festivities among the tenants at Chowbent to celebrate the marriage of Edith Powys.

## ATHERTON IN 1824

Baines, the industrious historian of the county in 1824 compiled a historical directory of Lancashire townships, which preserves detailed information on trades, inns, manufactures, schools, carriers and often by a key of numbers identifies the location of his lists of individuals. This important record of local significance has been reproduced in full. He gives the six inns set in neighbour rivalry on the busy turnpike roads near the chapel of St. John. Henry Shepherd of the Woolpack acted as chapel clerk. Rev. E. A. M. Booth occupied the parsonage as deputy for old Foxley and Benjamin Rigby Davis increased his income by a private school. James Thorp was town crier and at Alder House dwelt

Ann Withington. There were 17 active nailors, 5 with their own sales shops. Atherton at this time counted 4,145 souls; ahead lay bounding prosperity in coal and cotton. Baines has left us his picture faithful in every detail on the very threshold of this historic era.

## GREEN BANK, 1824

This substantial house was listed in 1824 as a boarding school, then under the care of Miss S. Pearson. By 1853 David Hodgkinson, Lord Lilford's steward, had left Platt Fold to live at Green Bank. He died here in 1854, aged 63. In 1891 James Kirkpatrick, son of Thomas who was a cotton mill owner, is found at Green Bank. His sister Anne was the wife of Caleb Wright.

## THE DEMOLITION OF ATHERTON NEW HALL, 1824

The folly of mad Richard Atherton ceased to adorn the local landscape in this year. Lord Lilford decided to pull it down, for he found its upkeep costly and as much expense had been lavished on Bewsey, it was considered one Lancashire residence was enough. The Hall had at times been occupied by members of the Powys family and sometimes by one of the land agents. Hodgkinson himself once lived here. Hardly a century old, the building came to the end of its life. The furniture, carpets and other appointments were sent to Bewsey and the clock in the Hall tower given to Chowbent chapel. In the spacious gardens and woodlands were peacocks and not far away an ornamental lake spanned by a beautiful bridge with stone lions leading to an avenue of trees and so to the very centre of Leigh, its church and market, where heavy gates, ponderous and padlocked, barred access to all except a privileged few. On January 1, 1828, Elizabeth Legh Kirk, sister of Lady Lilford, wrote to Chowbent asking Hodgkinson to preserve for her the cornices and ceilings of the best rooms and send them by Pickfords from either Manchester or Warrington to Stoughton Grange in Leicestershire. But Hodgkinson had to tell her that it was too late. For after the auction the demolition men moved in and all was quickly demolished. As

Hodgkinson had lived in the Hall, he was somewhat sad. His letter describes it as a noble mansion and ends "Peace be to its manes".

## ST. JOHN'S CHAPEL ORGAN, 1824

There was a grand and costly organ in Atherton Hall, a tribute witness to the accomplished culture of the great house. Hodgkinson was directed by Lord Lilford in 1824 to advertise it for sale. He did so with commendable diligence telling all and sundry the excellent qualities of the instrument. It was in this period that gallery minstrels in churches were ceding to the better attraction of full-throated organs and several from St. John's chapel came to Hodgkinson to beg for the organ as a gift and they would bear the expense of removal and setting up. But his lordship had in the interim promised the instrument to his sister-in-law, who was the wife of the rector of Winwick and to Winwick church it went. Nothing discouraged, a subscription list was opened to which Atherton townsmen gave quite substantial sums and a new organ was bought from Bewsher and Fleetwood for £250. Hodgkinson himself contributed, and in May 1825 he wrote to his master an account of the two services at which it was first played. The collections even came to £60. Though the organ had been bought outright, it was decided that this sum should form the basis of a fund to pay for an organist. Certain pew rents were set aside to augment this and Richard Norris was appointed at a salary of £15 a year.

## ATHERTON POST OFFICE, 1824

Letters for Atherton came by the mail coaches to a centre like Warrington. There the main bag was sorted and letters for Leigh sent by the lesser coach, where the foot post took them to the outlying districts. They were usually left at some inn, until they were called for. Letters for important persons like Hodgkinson were delivered to the house. The date stamp bears the price charged, which varied according to the distance. With the rise of travel and trade a post office was fixed at Atherton before 1824.

It was in Bolton Road with Robert Salter as master. When the penny postage was introduced Ann Cowburn was in charge. She was traceable as late as 1853, when George Hewitt probably succeeded her. He occurs in 1861. A later master, when the office was to be found in Market Street, was Harry Boreham. As the town grew in importance, a crown office was built in Crabtree Lane. Besides this main block, there are three sub-branches operating.

## ATHERTON WORKHOUSE, 1824

Atherton supported its own workhouse, as did all the six townships of the ancient parish. It was in Hagfold. William Bent was the governor and the cost of keeping the inmates was met by rates levied by the overseers of the poor. Atherton workhouse continued to the year 1837, when the townships in face of rising costs of administration combined with Culcheth and Lowton to form the Leigh Union. In 1850 the buildings known as Atherleigh were erected on land sold to the guardians by Lord Lilford for £640. Jeremiah Brimelow, an inmate of the workhouse had died suddenly and the county coroner held an inquest. His fee book under date September 6, 1819, shows that he travelled a distance of sixteen miles to view the body and the cost of the proceedings was £1 12*s*.

## LORD LILFORD'S BANKERS, 1825

Personal property and assets at this time were administered on a diocesan basis. Lancashire money and moveables belonging to Lord Lilford were accountable to Chester, those at Lilford to Peterborough, and in London to the bishops' court there. Hodgkinson, as the agent of his busy absent master, banked the receipts of the Atherton estates in the bank of Jones Loyd & Co. in King Street, Manchester, those of the Bewsey estates at Warrington in Parr Lyon and Greenhall. At Warrington his lordship had £4,152 13*s*. 7*d*., and at Manchester £3,298 14*s*. 11*d*. For the materials of Atherton Hall Hodgkinson had received £1,116 of which £200 was still unpaid. All these sums of money had now to be sent to Martin's bank in the capital.

## RALPH FLETCHER QUANTIFIES THE COAL MEASURES, 1825

In a letter sent to Hodgkinson, Fletcher informed him that for the past four years on an average 7,268 tons of coal had been got from Atherton pits. He reckoned that under 1,684 Cheshire acres a seam one yard in thickness would produce 8,000,000 tons. At the rate of getting from 1821 to 1825 this would last 1,100 years. Even, he said, if the production went up fivefold that would be 220 years. It was a shrewd projection of his calculating mind into an unknown future. But with steam power the lift tonnage reached astronomical figures. In 1913 alone it was 670,000 tons. By 1965 the last pit in Atherton ceased to produce and a fabulous age of coal came to an abrupt end.

## THE SECOND LORD LILFORD, 1826

Thomas Powys, second Lord Lilford, succeeded his father in 1800 and died in 1825. By his marriage at Penwortham in 1797 with Henrietta Maria, the heiress daughter of Robert Vernon Atherton, he acquired all the Atherton estates. Like his father, he was sent to Eton and graduated from St. John's, Cambridge, in 1797. He followed the legal traditions of the house of Powys and was called to the bar by Lincoln's Inn. The Prerogative Court of Canterbury preserves his will, by which he gave to his eldest son, Thomas Atherton Powys, the mansion house at Lilford, all books, linen, stores, wines, livestock and deer, and all turnpike securities in Northamptonshire and Lancashire. His trustees had to sell the leasehold Grosvenor Square house, with the coach houses, stables, pictures, china and books to pay all his debts and invest the surplus in public stocks for the benefit of younger sons and daughters. One interesting bequest of £200 was to the estates steward John Selby and to his son Thomas, who was his lordship's godson, £200, and a like sum to Richard Hodgkinson. By codicil he directed allotment of £300 to the eldest daughter, Henrietta Maria, £250 to the second daughter, £150 to the third, and to the others only £50. Close relatives of the family received 10 guineas to buy memorial rings and £20 for the poor in the parishes of Northamptonshire. The total estimate of his moveables in Chester diocese, excluding those in the province of Canterbury, was under £18,000

## THE AGE OF THE RAILWAY, 1828

This great age came early to Atherton, for the Bolton-to-Leigh railway was opened on August 1, 1828. An engine had been built by Stephenson at Newcastle-on-Tyne. It was brought to Pendlebury Fold in Hulton, put on the rails, with six wagons full of notables, another seven with ladies and gentlemen and the Bolton Old Band playing music. Mrs. Hulton christened the engine "The Lancashire Witch" and the demoniac power of the new steam engine proceeded at 12 miles per hour. Later it was demonstrated how much weight of coal it could pull. Although passengers were carried on this day, which was soon to change the face of the whole world, the line was used mainly for coal. Passengers came later after the success of the Manchester-Liverpool line. The bell of the engine was long preserved at Hulton Hall. So successful was the venture that the line was extended to join up with the more famous railway at Kenyon junction. Bag Lane station and Railway Hotel owe their existence to the Bolton and Leigh railroad, which later formed part of the London and North Western system. In 1864 came the Eccles-Wigan line, with a station originally called Chowbent, but later Howe Bridge. The last rail developed by the Lancashire and Yorkshire was in 1889 with Central Station as its stop. The insistent and inexorable pressure of the motor-car and lorry led to the decline of this mode of transport and Bag Lane and Howe Bridge stations were dismantled and the lines taken up.

## THOMAS HORROCKS OF ATHERTON, 1827

His will describes him as a dissenting minister and schoolmaster. He was tenant of Lord Lilford under a three-lives lease. He gave to Manchester College, which had then removed to York, £200. At this time Benjamin Rigby Davis was minister at Chowbent, which was then a Protestant Presbyterian Dissenting Chapel and Horrocks left £100 for the benefit of the present and future ministers. The leasehold estate had to be sold and the money distributed among seven named relatives. Davis took all his books and papers.

## LORD LILFORD'S SHOOT, 1828

With the demolition of Atherton Hall in 1824, on those occasions which obliged Lord Lilford to come north from Oundle, he stayed at Bewsey. He lodged there in 1828, when he had bought the shooting rights over 17,000 acres of Scottish moor. Hodgkinson, his faithful agent, crossed over to Warrington with many estate matters to discuss, one of which was a renewal of the lease of a former master of Leigh free school, James Blundel.

## CHOWBENT CHAPEL TRUST DEED, 1829

When the chapel moved to its new location near Alder House, a trust deed of the land and burial yard gave to certain elders of the congregation the legal estate, but as years went on no trace of this grant could be found. A sale of Alder House by the heirs of Nathan Mort never included the chapel site and yard. The school deed of 1734 mentions certain persons who could have been the original trustees of the chapel in 1722. There were fifteen in all and whenever that number fell below five, another deed was to be made. Laxity was ever the rule in such matters. In 1829 it was discovered that the last surviving trustee, John Mort, was dead and his two daughters joined in a new deed vesting the site and endowments in a fresh conveyance to fifteen stalwarts of the chapel community.

## RALPH FLETCHER, 1832

He died in this year, leaving a widow, three sons and four daughters. John Fletcher the eldest was 25: he took the pits in Lever. Ralph was 17 and set for the university. Their father divided the Atherton pits into six shares, three for John, two for Ralph and his brother James aged 13, and the last share for a nephew, John Langshaw, brought up by Mr. Fletcher. The widow Jane was left £600 a year. The executors he chose were this Jane, Ellis Fletcher, Joseph Green, John Langshaw and the ever-trusted Richard Hodgkinson. The personal estate was returned at under £14,000. Fletcher never lived in Atherton: he died at the Hollins within Haulgh, Bolton.

## BAPTIST CHAPEL, 1832

For long centuries there had been two prominent religions in Atherton, Presbyterian and Anglican. The Moravians came in 1733 to the Harrison chapel and in 1832 the baptists began to meet in cottages in the Valley. The early pioneers were Ralph Swinburne, of Chequerbent, Henry Ranicar and John Jones, a carpenter "like his Master". They leased a site in Dan Lane and there built their meeting house, the chapel of Hephzibah. Its first pastor was David Thompson, who laid the sure foundations of the future by building a larger chapel. Thirty years later he returned as minister. Thompson's chapel was opened October 17, 1842. One early minister, Worrall, emigrated to the States. There was a vigorous Sunday school attached to the chapel with 211 scholars in 1854. The year 1868 was a landmark in the history of the congregation, for then Abraham Burrows and Elizabeth his wife became full members. Destiny made of them and the entire family some of the finest benefactors any house of prayer could nominate. After long sessions of deliberation it was decided to rebuild the chapel and in 1904 the present church was opened; it cost £7,050 and like the parish church it was an outward sign of the prosperity of the township, without doubt at that era the most opulent of industrial communities within the county palatine. A new manse was provided for the minister opposite to Hulton Park gates and the old residence converted into houses, one for the schoolmaster and the other for the chapel keeper. In 1910 came the Ridgway Hall built to meet the social needs of the growing congregation from a benefaction by Mrs. Ridgway. At this period the stipend of a single minister was £120 and if married £130. Prosperity continued to favour the church and in 1917 the freehold title to all the site was acquired from Lilford Estates. From a long line of elected pastors emerge the names of two crowned with distinction: Malins Johnson, who wrote the centenary chapel history in 1932, and W. D. Hudson, who took a doctorate in theology and on leaving Atherton became a teaching member of Exeter University.

## ALBION MILL, 1834

It was built in this year by Thomas Manley and Philip Newton, both nailmasters, on a part of Knight's farm. The lease was for 99 years and the rent £11 14*s*. Additional land for a reservoir was later taken. In December 1889 fire destroyed the cotton mill, which was never restored. The Atherton Local Board, beset with many problems which the town's rapid growth had occasioned, moved under their compulsory powers to acquire the site for a sewage works and an isolation hospital. But local residents, 79 of them signed a petition, showed their opposition to these alarming proposals, including R. Stothert & Sons of Albion House, Bag Lane. Eventually Atherton council joined with Leigh in the matter of sewerage and with neighbouring authorities in setting up an isolation hospital at Astley. John Norbury later acquired the mill, from Samuel Newton, who died in 1847.

## ATHERTON GAS WORKS, 1835

Early gas works were promoted by private companies. About this year gas appeared as a feature of progress and ordered development in Atherton. It proved to be such an asset to the growing town that a defined area known as the "gas district" was recognized as being superior to the rest of the locality. Further distant townsfolk were taking gas from Leigh and the dependence of this part of the old township on Leigh for such services was one of the reasons set out for detaching part of Atherton and putting it to the new borough in 1899. Pressures of progress and thrusts of population effected these changes of pre-conquest boundaries. Atherton Gas Company provided an indifferent service; the quality and price of the gas caused many complaints and in 1872 the local board purchased the entire undertaking. James Peake was an early manager.

## THE EPISCOPALIAN AND UNITARIAN CHAPELS, 1835

The ministers at both these chapels were very advanced in age. Foxley was at the Atherton chapel; no one knew his exact age, but he was rising 90. To ease the burden of pastoral work he paid Mr. Booth to help his assistant, Samuel Johnson, who on his death became his successor. Foxley went to live at Hindley and then moved to Radcliffe. He came on occasion to preach at Atherton, but the minister's house was falling into disrepair. Few people came to his new chapel and the receipt of pew rents fell lower and lower. In fact so low that the chapel clerk could not get his wages of £6 14*s.* per annum paid and they were in arrear from 1828. At Chowbent chapel conditions were the same. Davis, the minister there, had done nothing for a whole year. He died in 1835 and there was a lapse of some time before a new minister took up duty. Hodgkinson reported all this to his master and told him many Atherton townsfolk went to the new church built in 1824 upon the Tyldesley Banks.

## BENJAMIN RIGBY DAVIS, 1835

So he wrote his own name on the will of Henry Leyland in 1815. He was minister of God's Word at Chowbent Chapel for 43 years. At his death he was aged 66 and originated from Wigston in Leicestershire. Wright in his *Story of Chowbent Chapel* gives a portrait of him in his prime.

## "THE CHOWBENT HERO", 1837

To get to Manchester in this year of grace the townsfolk of Atherton used the coach, which left the yard of the White Horse at Leigh at 7 a.m. every Tuesday morning and passed through Chowbent. This coach was so called in honour of Parson Wood. A second coach called "The Wonder" did the same journey on each Saturday at the same time. The fare was 4*s.* return. When Atherton was linked up by rail through Chowbent Station this mode of ancient travel disappeared from the turnpike roads. The same competition drove out of business the goods carrier, Thomas Hope of Atherton Fold.

## STREET LIGHTING, 1837

A group of ratepayers in this year attempted to adopt the Lighting Acts and get the streets of Atherton lit with the new illumination, gas. But the opposition was too strong; in 1844 the progressives tried again and the vote for was narrowly defeated by a very small number. Murdoch in 1805 had lit a Salford cotton mill with gas and the superiority of the new form over candles was in question. Some early mills in Atherton had their own gas plant. Later the opposition was overcome and Atherton's roads were illuminated by gas, until the advent of electricity at the beginning of the 20th century, when the Lancashire Transport Company supplied bulk power to the urban district and many private subscribers in both Atherton and Tyldesley.

## THE ASSESSMENT BOOK OF 1838

Township administration is mirrored and reflected in this book, drawn up in the same year as Thomas Kearsley caused one to be made for Tyldesley. For in it all owners, occupiers and rateable values are given. It is itself a witness to the change which was being developed in local government. Population and problems were increasing and the old framework was proving inadequate. Paid officers in full control and high capital costs were needed to meet the pressures of change. Instead of working the statutory days on the roads, there appears an official, paid a salary, with men on his roll to do the work required. Those who still adhered to the old system were allowed to labour often with their carts, but the advantages of the new methods were quickly seen. The majority saw that paying a composition instead of doing the repairs and improvements to the local roads was far more convenient. In the 1838 book John Fletcher's Gib Field pit was rated at £750, the highest in the town. His other collieries were valued at £208. The Gib Field was known as the Great Mine on tickets of sale issued by the banksman Higson. Rated with the mines was a counting house, weigh machine and wheelwright's shop. No other mines were operative at this time in Atherton. The cotton mills were those belonging to Manley & Newton—the factory, scutching room, loom shade, steam engine and gearing, all of which were rated at £177 13*s*. 6*d*. Although the town had its own gas plant, this mill possessed its own producer to light the mill in winter; it had progressed out of the age of the candle. Alfred Sylvester's factory was of a value of £137 11*s.* 6*d.* Here was found the building, the devil room, staircase shed, engine and boiler house, gearing, reservoir, truck house and a separate dwelling for one of the officials. Sylvester's workfolk bought their provisions at the truck shop. After Gib Field pit the next highest rated property was the Bolton and Leigh railway at £460 2*s.* 10*d.* Industry was inexorably pushing the value of properties in the town to high new levels. Lord Lilford's tithes still stayed at their old estimate of £73 6*s.* 8*d.* and the unitarian school and schoolhouse figures at £3 9*s.*

## JOHN HARRISON, 1838

He came as a young scholar bachelor to Chowbent chapel in 1838 and left in 1847 to begin a London ministry at Brixton. Educated at Manchester College, York, he studied for a time at the small university of Giessen in Hesse-Darmstadt, where he took the German degree of Ph.D. A son of his, William Gowland Harrison, gave a sum of £2,000 to increase the stipend of the chapel minister, with a proviso that if any incumbent had to relinquish his duties by reason of ill-health, he was to receive a half of the income for the duration of his life.

## THE NUT AND BOLT INDUSTRY, 1839

From the making of nails to the manufacture of nuts and bolts is not a great development; the skills which made Chowbent nailors famous in the north of England caused them to turn to new products of their ingenuity which the machine age of the industrial revolution had evolved. For some nailors in their smithies and rocks had turned to making spindles, healds and flies; it is said that the great Samuel Crompton himself, when baffled by one of his many problems, came to Chowbent with a special drawing of a part he wanted to fit in with his mule. Thomas Blakemore was one of the early innovators of this new industry, growing gradually out of the old. He had his rock in

Bag Lane, but with tradition and conservatism on his side, he still kept to nails and sold them in the shop attached to his house. He was active and prosperous in 1853 and by 1880 had formed his own company on a master's scale. Demand for rivets, bolts and screws grew with the expanding years of the century and inevitably the rising market of these ousted the nail trade. By 1853 there were eight makers of nuts and bolts; among them were James Prestwich and Robert Parker, both neighbours in Bag Lane. In 1869 there were eleven; Edward Davies at Collier Brook. He had been in the trade several years before 1853. In 1869 Carr and Nichols are listed. By 1880 Thomas Smith in Dan Lane, Johnson and Davies in Bolton Old Road, James Barnes in Bag Lane, and John Bullough, who had been active since 1856. Small companies like the Bolton Bolt and Nut Company which, changed to the Union Bolt, was set up in Wigan Road. Later on in the course of time Blakemores became part of the huge Guest, Keen and Nettlefold group, while the two family firms of Prestwich and Parker joined to form one single company.

## ST. JOHN'S CHAPEL IN 1839

Agent Millin Selby informed Lord Lilford about the state of Atherton. He claimed the chapel would seat 1,000 and that out of this number there were only 35 free seats; he recommended all seats should be free. The Sunday school was flourishing: 240 girls, 150 boys, average attendance of 180 and 100 respectively. Unitarians and baptists supported these types of school, which taught the rudiments of reading, spelling and writing. There were day schools; in those run by the established church 116 scholars, and in the dissenting 161. There was a school for infants, daily average 54 out of a possible 80.

## ATHERTON IN 1840

In this year a composite picture of the town begins to emerge in considerable detail from the trade directories. It was about to develop its broadbased foundations on coal and cotton, which would constitute the mainstay of its population and wealth for above a century to come. John Fletcher and his partners were active in coal mining on the Hindley boundary of the town. Cotton manufacturers comprised for the most part small individual undertakings owned by Mary Diggle, Thomas Grundy, James Hesketh, Edward Bernard Holland, Joseph and Edward Ramsbotham, which three were in Bag Lane, and Arthur Silvester. These two industries were soon to eclipse all others of the neighbourhood and cause a rise in population fourfold in numbers. From now on the nail industry takes a subordinate place; it was still well rooted in Chowbent and in 1840 there were at least twenty-two nailors, whose names are given in an appendix.

## THE NATIONAL SCHOOL, 1840

This early school was built on land donated by Lord Lilford along Market Street; its site area was half an acre. The conveyance of October 14, 1840, vested the land in the name of the curate Samuel Johnson and others and the school opened on September 14, 1841. A stone inscription told the passer-by: "This school was erected AD 1840 by Subscription from members of the Established Church aided by a grant from the Committee of Council on Education". The school developed on the usual pattern of national schools, boys separated from girls and a separate infants department. The first master was David Broadbent, with his wife in charge of the girls. He taught for 30 years and both retired in 1871. The local name of the school was Lane Top school. In 1851 a school house was built, Edward Dean was the last to live in it as master. He left in 1895; then the teacher of the infants, Jane Twist, occupied it until 1921, when it was converted into a boys' cloakroom and staff rooms. Earlier, in 1902, the school had been enlarged during the teaching years of Timothy Belshaw, who resigned in 1924. It was then that the school, after being co-educational for many years separated again with Edward Ramsbottam as head and Miss McLean in charge of the girls. The year 1932 produced the greatest change of all. New additions were made to make the school a senior school for pupils over eleven while the juniors were sent to Hindsford or Howe Bridge schools. The name chosen to differentiate this senior school was Hesketh Fletcher, memorializing in a fitting way the names of Sarah Hesketh and the Fletcher family, benefactors to the cause of education in Atherton. In 1968 this old school saw the end of its long life. A new modern building was erected along Hamilton Street and the site of the Lane Top school was sold.

## LOCAL GOVERNMENT IN THE 19TH CENTURY

Atherton's unique series of township records enables a full picture to be drawn of the way in which local affairs were managed just before the adoption of the Act of 1858. With the decay of ancient manorial organization, the coming in of new problems, the need of great capital outlay, a modern system had to be evolved. Annual meetings of ratepayers were announced by notices given out by Thomas Sale, the chapel clerk, in Chowbent chapel or by posters affixed to the two chapel doors, and the meeting place was the old school, to choose one example, at 10 o'clock in the morning, the day, August 9, the year 1838. There was no annual chairman; one was named by a show of hands for the present occasion. Agenda included selection of constables, overseers of the highways, churchwardens and guardians of the poor. Usually lists were prepared beforehand. The location of the old school could only be the ancient grammar school; the only other school was the national, which was then far from being old. A town's office was available in the Public Hall, built soon after the new road to Bolton was laid down. When the old schoolroom ceased to exist, the annual meeting was held in the vestry of St. John's, but more often at the Bear's Paw inn. The principal part of the business was to pass first the accounts of the different officers, to see that, in the colourful language of that day, they made "even" with the town. Some of the substantial attenders signed the accounts as correct. In 1842 the aged Richard Hodgkinson was voted to the chair; William Fildes was re-elected surveyor at his usual salary of £15 per annum. New perplexities were beginning to appear. The valuation of the Bolton-to-Leigh railway had been made; the occasion had never risen before and as the line went right through the town, adjacent lands were considerably enhanced in value. The company objected to the high guessed-at figure; an appeal to Kirkdale Sessions resulted and the need for the services of a professional valuer in George Gorton of Bury arose. There was no general rate. A poor rate of 1*s*. in the £ was a static demand for several years, with a rate called for the roads much less. Owners of cottage properties paying rates received back the generous allowance of one-third. Though the minutes are sometimes slender in content, they illuminate the history of the town in different ways. One entry in 1844 tells that Ralph Fletcher was taking part in local affairs and living at the Hillock. He was a guardian of the poor in 1852 and for many succeeding years. About this time the county was building up the basis of a rate. Empty properties exempt were a source of trouble with special committees set up to examine them. New names of outstanding men begin to appear for the first time—James Burton and Caleb Wright. By 1856 the annual meeting was being called in the National School, where they regularly convened until the Public Hall was built on the new road.

## NEW PROBLEMS OF LOCAL GOVERNMENT

Many new problems confronted the growing town and its officials during the 19th century. The growth of population threw the chapel yards and the old churchyard at Leigh into conflict with urgent crises. A burial board was appointed to deal with this as early as 1852. Then a nuisance committee appears in 1856 to cover new risks to health. Increased traffic on the road brought opposition to the tollbars, one of which was in the very centre at the market place. Progress demanded they should be swept away. A meeting voted that the town take over the upkeep of the highway from Punch Bowl to the Bear's Paw and from the new cemetery to the stocks, so that only one bar remained, at Kirkhall Lane. The Act of 1858 was adopted in 1863 and early in 1864 the first election of members to a new local board was made. As always there were objections. It was moved that the Act be restricted to an area known as the gas district, but the final resolution was that it apply to the township as a whole. A new consciousness was afloat and population and wealth were striding fast ahead. In 1873 a strong-box was purchased to protect the town records and the key entrusted to a churchwarden. Edward Manley was paid 2 guineas to arrange them in order and catalogue them.

## EARLY INVESTMENT IN THE COTTON TRADE, 1804

The industry in its early stages embraced a great number of small manufacturers, who erected sheds and had to supply most of the capital for machinery themselves or by partners. Many of these early factory owners were far from rich. The widow of James Edge, who died in 1807, had less than £100. The great fortunes came later and so did the leviathan structures of cavernous mills, which were soon to dominate an industrial landscape. One early investment was £65 10*s.* to Part and Gregory, spinners on Tyldesley Banks lent to them by William Croft, wheelwright of Atherton. Croft left this to his wife Ellen. It was an early instance of a capital loan in an industry soon to develop into one of the richest any country had ever seen.

## THE THOMAS HARRISON CHAPEL, 1804

This was a small conventicle house built by Thomas Harrison, who appears listed in the 1792 directory. In 1804 a weaver, John Young, gave a freehold house in Atherton to the trustees of this chapel who were to pay 20*s.* a year to a teacher instructing a "quantity" of scholars attending there each Sunday. Young's good sense is a commentary upon the importance played in democratic education arising out of Raikes' Sunday Schools. He saw the weakness of voluntary service and wished to reward a teacher who elected to give of his or her time. But he stipulated that no less than 40 should be on the class register and further that the best six scholars should have a Bible, price 5*s.*, given to them on Christmas morning yearly and every year for ever. The trustees appointed were to purchase a ledger to enter up the receipts of the house and garden and if the income exceeded 50*s.* the excess was to be applied for the purchase of linen and woollen cloth for the poor. If the Harrison chapel proved troublesome to the trustees by not allowing the use of the building as a schoolroom they were to approach the Chowbent chapel and apply the income for the same purpose. Young owned a part of Alder Fold and belonged to that family long associated with Great Fold in Bedford.

## WILLIAM ECKERSLEY, 1807

He was host of the King's Head before 1792 to the year of his death in 1807. Besides being innkeeper, he had leased four fields off Bag Lane to help him as husbandman. He was well-to-do and able to cancel a large debt of £514 to the husband, Edmund Manley, of his stepdaughter Jane and still provide £400 for his own sister Mary, wife of chapman Nicholas Cunliff. For he had property leases in Westhoughton, Ince-in-Makerfield, Tyldesley, Middle Hulton, and in the Valley in Atherton a house occupied by John Peake. Eckersley left 10 guineas as a small tribute of respect to John Swift, a surgeon in Atherton at this time. His five cottages in Dan Lane were tenanted by Robert Bradshaw, William Pemberton, John Sidlow, William Caldwell and widow Jarratt. King's Head inn had several outbuildings, a carthouse, shippon and two stables and a bowling green. All stock in trade, horses, cattle, furniture, plate and linen were to be realized and the money invested for the children of his three sisters to bring in an income for each of £20. After Eckersley's death the inn passed into the possession of the Manleys. Edmund Manley is listed here in 1824. By 1853 the King's Head offered a news room, where local papers then in circulation could be read by the customers. Ann Manley was hostess. Then in 1869 James Horrobin, Joseph Whalley in 1895, and Walter Kay, 1909.

## WIDOW CANNON'S HOUSE, 1807

Her detailed will provides for posterity a full picture of the interior of her Chowbent home. She preferred mahogany pieces and had only one chest of drawers in good native oak. Dining table, desk, bookcase, card table, were all fashioned in this exotic wood. Around the main table were set six spindle-back chairs; on the walls pictures, mirror and weather glass. The range with its pilkin, pans and bakers was styled the chimney piece. On the dining table there sparkled silver and not yeoman's pewter. There were silver tea-spoons, silver tankard, silver cream jug and sugar tongs; upstairs a blue and white check bed and bedding, another, the best blue and white printed bed, and a smaller one. Even the pepper box had to be silver. To complete her list of possessions, carpets, linen, glasses, china. hair trunk, and an umbrella.

## THE WOOLPACK, 1808

Thomas Standbank had some interest in this ancient tavern; he is noted in the big manor court book as having to do service for it both in this year and in 1838. But Baines lists with precision Henry Shepherd as innkeeper in 1824. Most of the inns nestling in the shadow of St. John's chapel had fostered some association with that community and Shepherd was chapel clerk there. It was he whose salary fell in Foxley's time much in arrear. Mary Bradshaw and Ann Markland occur in 1853 and 1869 and Edward Warburton in 1895

## ATHERTON COURT BARON, 1808

The lord of the manor had the right immemorial to hold a court in Atherton at which all his tenants attended to do suit and service. One such court was known as the court baron and the other the court leet. The first dealt with matters touching the estate, the farms, tenancies, ditches, footpaths and nuisances. The court leet took cognizance of assaults, debts, ownership disputes, vagrancy and lodging houses. Fines imposed by these two courts were in times past a source of profit to the Athertons and their successors. Eventually the income and issues declined and the courts were abandoned. Records of the court leet are wanting. But those of the court baron have survived among the Lilford muniments from the year 1808 to 1888, when no more sessions were held. The court met in November of each year and appointed a jury with the foreman. Other officers were the scavengers, triers of weights and measures, burleymen, market lookers, afferors, billet master, bailiff, and constable. The court met at the King's Head Inn, where the estate audit took place. From 1844 it was deemed necessary to appoint a town crier, but this office of colour and folklore lapsed in 1870; James Hope was one of the last of his group. The jury heard the presentments. Burleymen covered trespasses by animals and had charge of the pound and its fences; Scavengers tidied the estate; the market lookers watched the market for tolls; the triers of weights and measures checked the sale of bread and ale; and afferors fixed the amount of fine. If a tenant did not attend, he was fined *2d.* From 1830 to 1888 a large court book contains the proceedings but only one item other than appointment of office holders and tenants' names is recorded, that of a badly constructed sewer in 1852. The court was convened regularly each year and all the officers appointed. The last court to be held was on November 7, 1888. Previous to 1838 the steward signed the business agenda as it was set down on sheets of foolscap. The steward for many years was John Gorst, followed by Richard Marsh of Westleigh.

## THE GARDENER AT ATHERTON HALL, 1808

The head gardener of the house of Lilford died June 13, 1808. By his long years of service he had been able to establish himself and was able to leave some £450 for his dependants. His name was William Slow and the accounts of the steward show that his wage was £52 per annum. He asked Hodgkinson to realize his effects and use part of the money to set up in the world the youngest son Joseph. His other sons were George and John; they had to pay back what they had borrowed from the father. A daughter Ellen, with her mother, shared the remainder. She was at the age of 16 apprenticed to Rachel and Mary Dracup of Bolton as a mantua maker. The son John enlisted and was a private in the 1st Regiment of Dragoons.

## PRESENTMENTS AT THE COURT BARON, 1808–27

Charges laid before the jurors of Atherton during these years define the extent of the powers which the court wielded. The bailiff executed the orders signed by the steward. In 1808 James Murray was bailiff. James Mann had stopped up the watercourse from Abigail Aldred's garden and he was given 14 days to open it up. Ellen Pollitt had put two stoops in the roadway in front of her house and had to remove them. In 1810 Henry Seddon's pigs had roamed on to John Shaw's land and if the nuisance occurred again he was to pay 30*s*. Next year more business was before the court. Roger Eckersley of Car Bank was ordered to repair the footbridge in Sandpit field. His cattle too had been at large on the potato crops of many complaining tenants. The burleymen had estimated the damage at 35*s*. Chowbent-to-Shakerley footpath was in a bad state and Thomas Brimelow and William Sanderson had to effect a repair or otherwise pay 39*s*. James Wood had not scoured his ditch. Lovers Lane path to Pickley Green was foundrous and Richard Hope had six weeks to improve it. Chanters footpath was reported upon in 1812 and Richard Halliwell named as liable to repair it. From these proceedings it will be seen that the court occupied itself with estate management for the community as a whole and that this side of its useful activity passed in time to the local elected council set up by the statutes of the 19th century.

## MANOR HOUSE, 1808

The house existed many years before this time, when John Sale died here in 1808. He left the house to his wife Ann. Sale had two smithies, which he let to the younger Richard Manley and when the lease expired his bellows and tools were to be sold and the money divided betwixt his brother Richard and his nephews. John Eckersley, innkeeper, and Thomas Collier, nailmaster, were two of his friends he trusted to see these dispositions carried out. Later in 1864 William Hesketh was at Manor House. He was elected to the first Atherton Council set up after the passing of the Local Government Act of 1858.

## THE WEAVER'S SHILLING, 1810

Richard Clowes was a weaver at outs with his wife. Knowing his hour was fast approaching, he cut her off with a shilling. That was all Mary, who had borne him one son John, was to have. Clowes's mother had to collect the rents from Thorps Cottages and pay them to her grandson.

## THE EPISCOPAL CHAPEL REBUILT, 1810

That small brick edifice of 1645 had become in time too small and in 1810 it was decided to pull it down. A larger chapel was built on part of the site of the old, farther away from the main street. This second chapel had two galleries, with rented pews, praying places for 823. The minister took rents from 252, Lord Lilford 221, and to support the choir 100. But here was a source of recurring trouble. Since 1723 the Athertons, Gwillyms and Powys in their day had paid for most of the expense in running the chapel. They met the cost of repairs, the communion cloths, washing of the surplice, coal for the vestry fire, the bell, sacramental wine, furniture, oil for the rope, and the sexton's wages. Whenever the great Bible or the prayer book was worn out, they replaced it. But all this was out of the pew rents and from them the patron made a profit. The usual yearly rent for a pew was one guinea, collected personally by the agent in the chapel after service. The cost of this second chapel, built by Mr. Rothwell of Bolton, was £2,575 5*s.* 8*d.* Bricks used came to 210,000, sand 104 loads, 2,000 ft. of oak at £400 and 400 ft. of lime at £50. Matthew Lythgoe made the steeple, stairs and floor at a cost of £45 2*s.* 8*d.* At some later time the congregation bought an organ, paid for gas lighting, and collected to defray the wages of the organist and the chapel clerk.

## THE LUDDITES, 1812

New machines had been installed in a Westhoughton factory driven by steam, and cottage handloom weavers faced a bitter future. In Nottingham a half-wit called Ludd led a movement which it was hoped would solve the problem—destroy the machines, which had made them unemployed. The idea spread to Lancashire. On April 24, 1812, Job Fletcher, aged 34, of Atherton, Thomas Kerfoot of Westhoughton, aged 26, John Smith, aged 31, and Abraham Charlton, aged 14, burnt down the Westhoughton mill. At the Lancaster Assizes they were condemned to death and hanged on June 13. Sympathetic supporters tried to soften the harshness of this tragedy by sending a cart to Lancaster Castle to bring back their dead bodies to these parts. It returned empty.

## THE ECONOMICS OF A GIN PIT DURING THE YEARS 1803–7

A gin pit owned by Ralph Fletcher was winning coal on a very profitable basis during the war years 1803–7. Facts and great detail about its economic life are seen in the balance sheets which annually were sent to Lord Lilford, as owner of the royalties. It was a gin pit, worked by two horses and each horse cost £12 per annum to keep. Coal sales were kept in a separate ledger and each week the accounts showed whether there was a surplus or not. Weekly profits fluctuated violently. On August 16, 1806, the profit was 1½*d.*; on October 18 of the same year it reached £61 5*s.* 3*d.* And at the end of the balancing period one-quarter of the net profit was paid to Lord Lilford's agent. The mine used up a lot of timber and oak trees were bought from Greenhall and Coxes farms. Notwithstanding there was a Continental war the pit was able to buy in 1804 £73 worth of timber shipped from Danzig and Riga. John Pearson, the carpenter, made a ring of oak to hold up the shaft sides. In 1774 coal sold at 2*d.* per basket; in 1805 it had risen to 5*d.* and Fletcher asked Lilford to agree to his superintendence fee of the colliery to be raised from £31 a year to £52 to cover the increased work involved. The turnover in 1805 was £1,324 7*s.* 2*d.* Colliers after a special arduous job were told to go to the King's Head or the Bear's Paw and have free ale. Richardson sold on February 9, 1805, to the colliers £2 3*s.* 6*d.* of ale, which the pit paid for. Subsidence occurred on the turnpike road near to Greens and 250 yards of prop had to be bought on an emergency to support the road in October 1804. Next July the commissioners of the trust sold to the pit the materials of the old turnpike house for £10. It had become ruinous. Sale of coal was often paid for by bills and to get cash for these was costly. A fee of 12*s.* was charged to discount a £60 bill. Once a customer named Bullock sent in a bill which was returned as he was a bankrupt. Fletcher owned the Ladyshore pit at Rumworth and transferred from it a sinking rope on July 28, 1804. It was 60 yards long. The gin pit did other work besides getting coal. Brickmaking was profitable and carting of timber, lime, slate, thatch and flags helped on the rise of profits. Water was the main enemy of the underground roads. Soughs had to be constantly cleaned and in 1806 workmen cut a deep drain to carry water away from the Bent pits.

## THE CONSECRATION OF ST. JOHN'S CHAPEL, 1814

Though the chapel had been finished by 1811, there was delay in effecting its consecration. The bishop of Chester came on October 25, 1814, to declare the building fit for divine purposes. He read the communion service and the deed of consecration; Thomas Foxley, the curate, preached. When these formalities were finished, there were refreshments provided in the vestry. The bishop expressed himself satisfied with all he saw, complimented the singers upon the quality of their performance, and left at 4 p.m.

## MOURNING RINGS, 1814

This type of personal gift persisted in favour with testators for centuries. Shakespeare left such memorials to his friends. When widow Elizabeth Smith died in 1814, she gave a memorial ring to Chowbent chapel minister Davis and Mary his wife. Then she specified a black suit for her brother, Timothy Ingle, and a mourning suit for her servant, Hannah Whitton. Cousin Mary Ingle took a bombazeen, which was a twilled black dress. She showed her esteem for the chapel minister, long before his powers had declined, by leaving him £10 and making him an executor. A gold watch and seal went to a son, John Swift, and all other jewels and trinkets widow Swift had labelled as to where they should go. A niece, Ellen Ward, had her wedding ring. All she counted came to under £300.

## HILLOCK PIT, 1815

Three important officers controlled the early coalmines. The dialler surveyed operations under and above ground, the auditor kept the sales accounts, and the banksman was in charge of the surface brows. By October 1815 the life of the Hillock pit was at an end and most of the coal accessible from the shaft was worked out. Ralph Fletcher had some share in the mine and asked Hodgkinson, the Lilford agent, if he would agree to the banksman selling the coal on the Hill as the best way of bringing the pit's life to an end.

## THE LINEN DRAPER, 1815

Alexander Gordon kept a draper's shop on Chowbent for a long time. He had one son William, who became insane, and Margaret Leathwaite in 1815 gave his father £5 to be used for his benefit. Her own brother was afflicted in a like manner and to support him she set aside certain stock money, which if it came to be "unmade use of" was to be divided among others whom she named. Her will is colourful for its quaint Chowbent language, for at the foot of each sheet of her will is written in bold wording "Go forward" in place of "Please turn over".

## RED STREET, 1816

In this, one of the oldest of Chowbent locations, were five cottages tenanted by William Collier, George Rylance, James Charlson, and Margaret Halliwell. Spinster Ann Charlson owned them and with a silver tankard marked T.C. and a silver coffee pot and stand gave the row of houses to a nephew Thomas Collier. Beside the income of Red Street, she enjoyed the rents of six houses in Shakerley and part of a house in Eagle Street, London. Her nieces and nephews were her inheritors.

## HENRY ALRED AT THE BULL'S HEAD, 1817

He died at the inn in 1817 and had been there from before 1792. A list of his household goods confirms the taste shown by other Chowbenters of this era, their preference and pride in silverware. No other township of those which made up the old parish of Leigh reveals such quality of taste. For gone were the old wooden trenchers, and modest families were using Delft ware. In the Bull's Head inn were five silver teaspoons, four tablespoons, a silver punchbowl ladle, a tankard, a cup and an eight-day clock. Alred owned a rock smithy with all its gear; he left most of his £400 estate to two stepdaughters, Peggy Pollitt and Elizabeth Mollineux and John her son. The unique T. R. Weeton witnessed the will.

Thomas Pratt was a later landlord: he was at the inn in 1838. Baines gives T. Reddish in 1824, and in 1848 occurs James Kay.

## THE ENGINE PIT, 1802

Guests of Bedford were pioneers in the getting of coal. They were remarkable in other fields, medicine, surgery, cotton and brewing. In July 1802 John Guest asked advice of Thomas Livesey of Werneth Colliery, Oldham. For on the south-westerly side of Engine pit was a seam of coal 7 feet thick. It aroused the ingenuity of many minds how best to win it. There were several opinions. A survey had been made which estimated 124,200 cubic yards of solid coal, which by mine workings, and the creation of slack would reduce the saleable quantity by one-third. Each small pit on the coalfield had a probable life of 20 years; then it was necessary to bank again, in collier's language, dig a new shaft. But this was always costly and the owners of Engine pit thought of making a tunnel 1,000 yards long to New Atherton pit to take this good rich seam. The problem was the lift of the Engine pit. It required a power far beyond that of a gin engine to draw coal up the incline. The tunnel would cost £1,200–£1,500. A waterwheel with a powerful race and strong walling had been suggested, but Guest sought further advice. A waterwheel was cheap to run, but in a dry summer and in frost it was out of action. Livesey advised buying a 6-horsepower steam engine, cost £600–£650, which would draw water from the pit and lift from a depth of 70 yards and bring up three times more coal in a given period than any other method. The engine could be worked five hours out of the twenty-four and save a great expenditure on tunnelling, and being a moveable asset could be used again, when the seams were exhausted. Livesey proved right in his advice to Guest. It was the beginning of great things for the application of steam enabled deeper and deeper veins of black rich mineral to be mined.

## ISRAEL UNSWORTH, 1802

Israel was host at the Wheatsheaf, where Fletcher's colliers resorted for free ale after their arduous day's work in the pits. He had been genial landlord there for a long time and died in this year. He was assessed as being worth under £300 and owned three houses in Youth Lane and two in Dan Lane, which properties he left to his stepdaughter Ellen Pollitt and her daughter Ellen, wife of Peter Cleworth, equally.

## A PEW IN THE NEW CHURCH AT CHOWBENT, 1817

Samuel Gregory kept a shop in Atherton; nearby he had bought Berry's Cottages, where lived Margaret Sidlow, Mary Partington, James Collier, Thomas Sidlow, Joseph Eckersley, Henry Chorlton, Thomas Hall and William Whittaker, paying the rent. He owned a freehold in Westleigh, near to Kirkhall tollbar, on which was a dutch barn. His wife was Jane and his son Richard had died before him, leaving three natural children. He was worth £600 and when he went to the new church he sat in pew number 46, which he rented; it was in the north aisle. He trusted William McClure, fustian merchant of Tyldesley, and corn dealer William Shakeshaft of Chowbent to see to his affairs and look to the widow and the grandchildren. Gregory died August 1, 1817.

## LABURNUM HOUSE, 1818

The house was once located along Bolton Old Road; it was not an old house of the class of Chanters or Alder House. One early occupant was T. W. B. Sanderson in 1818, who was still here in 1864, and from 1881 to 1899 Thomas Hoyle Hope, a solicitor; he collected material about Chowbent chapel and Atherton township. The house gave its name to a cotton mill.

## COXES, 1818

Coxes was an old farmstead standing on the Atherton to Bolton highroad, tenanted in this year by Jeremiah Hodson. When Ellen Withington made her will in 1815 she had some share in Coxes. Early coalmines are located on Coxes land. A record of a prior century calls it Kixes. In 1864 Thomas Speakman was farming the holding.

## ATHERTON COLLIERIES AND THE CANAL TRAFFIC, 1818

No canal came near to Atherton; the Lilfords disliked such a project and steward Hodgkinson objected for them before a

Parliamentary Committee to the proposal by the Lancaster Canal Company in February 1794 to route a cutting across the Avenue and past Platt Fold. Later it was a matter of regret that water transport, so cheap for bulk materials, was remote from the pits at Atherton. The Duke of Bridgewater constructed his canal from Worsley to Leigh in 1795. The Leeds and Liverpool Canal Company joined up with their waterway at Pennington Bridge in 1819. The accounts of the Atherton Collieries in 1818 reveal some interesting payments, which show that the coalpits had linked up with water transport. In October of that year a boat was bought, which with delivery dues cost £30 6*s.* 4*d.* and the operating costs of two barges for tonnage and lock dues a month later was £6 13*s.* 2*d.* Later a payment is entered of £21 3*s.* 5*d.* for similar dues for seven boats. Drivers from the pits filled the empty barges at Limerick basin, but by surface transport it was very slow and costly. In 1858 Fletchers basin was made at the expense of the collieries to provide rail facilities for taking coal from Atherton to the canal. Part of this was underground in Chapel Street, Bedford.

## THE PRINCE COBURG INN, 1819

There has been a hostelry on this site from very early times. Formerly it was known as the Stag and as such it is listed in the 1792 directory. Later someone changed it to a name which is one of the most intriguing in the land. Alexander Heys was host in 1819 and the property was hanging on one life in being, that of John Woodward, aged 35, and the yearly rent was £20. On June 24 of the year 1819 the house and inn were auctioned. The conditions of sale were that at least three bidders were to be present, each bid had to be advanced by £2 and no less, and risks of fire, accident or death of the life in being were placed upon the purchaser One Samuel Newton purchased for £295; subsequently he sold to brewers, who set up William Shakeshaft as host. John Hodgkinson appears in 1824, Thomas Schofield in 1848 and 1853: then the long tenure of the McCabes, Michael in 1869, Thomas in 1895, and Elizabeth in 1909.

## BOLTON NEW ROAD, *c.* 1839

Sometime before this year a straight new high-level connecting road had been built from Bent Top to High Street and right across open country. Traffic from Bolton to Leigh was enabled to bypass the narrow lanes of the old township and the steep inclines of Bridge Foot so hard for horse-drawn vehicles. This new road threw Chowbent Chapel off the main beaten tracks. One of the first houses to be built along Bolton New Road in 1860 was Prospect House, for a long time the estate office for the Lilfords, which was later bought by the urban district for use as a surveyor's department. Then in 1860 came the first of the three mills of the Atherton Cotton Spinning Company. In course of time Bolton New Road became one of the most important of the roads in Atherton and by its justification inspired later the building of another high road, Tyldesley New Road. The tithe map of Atherton produced by the inquiry of this year shows the new highway already in use.

## ATHERTON VICARAGE, 1842

Curate Samuel Johnson leased the house known as the vicarage in Bee Fold Lane from Lord Lilford at a yearly rent of 8 guineas in 1842. He was already in occupation at the time the lease was made and it was to end with the expiration of his tenure of the office. The site area was 1 rood and 31 perches; additional a stable in Guest Fold and a field called Keepers Meadow, 4½ acres. Johnson was obliged to maintain the fences in good repair and attend at the local lord's court.

## LEIGH UNION, 1850

Each township had to provide some workhouse, where the inmates, if capable, were expected to work. Many details about conditions in Atherton workhouse are found in the surviving township papers. Soaring costs of the poor law caused in 1837 the six townships of the old parish of Leigh with Lowton and Culcheth to join together and form the Leigh Union. Atherton

## ATHERTON CEMETERY, 1857

Burial rights of Atherton's dead folk belonged to the mother church at Leigh. When the old Bent chapel in 1723 was consecrated the deed clearly stated that no burial or funeral sermon was to be allowed without leave of the vicar of Leigh. An ample graveyard surrounded the new chapel and burials took place there during the course of the 18th century. Plans of the episcopalian chapel rebuilt in 1814 show a small graveyard and even today memorial stones exist at the east end of the present church. But population growth in the last century soon exhausted all burial room for the dead and orders in council were made closing many churchyards and setting up burial boards to administer an essential service. In this way arose Atherton cemetery, where the first interment took place on February 15, 1857.

## CHOWBENT UNITARIAN SCHOOL, 1860

Minister Frankland, to signalize the centenary of "General" Wood's death in 1759, erected a building opposite the chapel, which was to be a Sunday and day school. An adjacent house of a higher pitch of roof served as a library. A day school was begun in 1860, which functioned to January 1871, when the trustees decided to put the school under Government inspection. They asked the master Mr. Haslam to resign in favour of Isaiah Barker, who began his long years of service, January 9, 1871, on a snowy morning. He had 72 scholars, worked with consistent enthusiasm and earned the first year a state grant of £61 9*s.* 4*d.* Receipts of school pence came to £1 3*s.* 4½*d.* The school prospered in stride with the growing population of the township and his staff increased. In 1873 the state grant was £135 6*s.* and 205 scholars enrolled. An assistant teacher in 1877 was paid £60 per annum; £40 a year was offered for an ex-pupil teacher mistress. Barker managed his growing school, infants, juniors and seniors, with three pupil teachers and a visiting mistress for sewing. Once he wrote in the public prints a letter in which he attacked a local cotton spinner for pressing half-timers to go to the church school. These juvenile workers paid 4*d.* per week as school money, which sometimes the factory master agreed to pay. In its early days had shared with Pennington before this date the upkeep of a poorhouse. In time the buildings became ruinous and in 1850 the guardians purchased land from Lilford in Atherton and built a new range of buildings. A later folk named the whole set of extensive blocks Atherleigh.

## BOTANICAL GARDENS, 1850

Victorians of industrial Lancashire spent their leisure in the study of botany. Clubs were formed, with a body of trustees to hold the corporate property and land acquired and often greenhouses erected. The cultural side included organized rambles on Chat Moss, lectures, study groups and preservation of all kinds of specimens. For a time these clubs flourished but, as with most societies, public interest declined and to survive many turned to the acquisition of a licence to sell spirits and beer and added billiards and bowling as more fashionable diversions. Such was the course of development of Atherton Botanical Gardens, which since about this year above has maintained an outlet for the leisure hours of many who have resorted to them over the years. Samuel Johnson was one of the many noted botanists at this parish.

## RICHARD STOTHERT, 1852

Stothert, for long a household name in Atherton, is not a native indigenous name. This firm of chemists was founded in 1852 and the shrewd Richard was new to these parts. He saw a fortune in pills and patent medicines at a time when sickness and absence from the mill and mine seriously disturbed the family income. And to sustain a moderate degree of health he began the manufacture in Albion House of a wide range of medicaments, which his itinerant travellers sold in all parts of the county. Richard Maxwell, his son, succeeded in the business; he died in 1947 and was in turn followed by his son. Latterly the firm turned to a new field, the manufacture of soft drinks and mineral waters. The change brought new prosperity and the entire firm was absorbed by another rival of the trade, Barrs of Glasgow.

## LEE STREET SCHOOL, 1871

The school occupies a unique place in Atherton history. Though associated closely in its influence with the nearby Baptist chapel, the school is not part of it and has always stressed by use of the word "undenominational" its detachment from allegiance to any particular sect. It was founded at that time when many schools in the township were forced into existence by the tremendous upsurge in population. Emma Snow was the first mistress, but the fortunes of the school, after two long closures, were consolidated by the mastership of F. G. Evans who began in 1903 and retired in 1940. From that year to 1952 A. V. Unsworth was head teacher, followed by J. H. Greenwood in 1953. The infants combined with the juniors in 1962. The seniors had been drafted under reorganization to other schools in 1932. Two scholars of Lee Street attained professorial status at Leeds University; one, a son of the headmaster, was M. G. Evans and his rival, John B. Speakman. Dorothy George, mistress in the infants school 1954–8 perished in the Barcelona air crash 1970.

## AN ERA OF PROSPERITY, 1872

Atherton Collieries entered about this time upon an era of lush prosperity. More powerful methods of raising coal were one of the causes which allowed rich and massive strata of coal to be mined, quite outside the reach of previous generations and staggering quantities of mineral gotten and won from 1872 onwards show a continual rise in profit and production. John Fletcher was the principal actor in this industrial drama. He was in Atherton before 1776 and active in the Lovers Lane Colliery. By 1872 the pits controlled by the Fletchers comprised not only this one, but the Victoria Seven Feet, the Chanters Seven Feet and Five Feet, the Crombouke and the Arley. Lovers Lane in 1881 raised 36,602 tons but this tonnage declined steeply as the years wore on. In 1891 it was only 14,280. The Fletchers, who shared this summer of unparalleled prosperity, embraced Ralph, Philip, George, Arthur John and Jane Fletcher, and the executors of the late Ralph Fletcher who watched the interests of infants Nellie and Wilfrid together with Jane Brandreth. Gross output for the year 1881 was 455,096 tons. This huge production continued on the upgrade till in 1913, the heyday time of the Lancashire coalfield, it topped 669,566 tons. The markets for this new wealth were Bolton, Liverpool, Warrington, Hartford, Manchester and the home area districts. Over the Bedford railway to the canal 42,164 tons alone were shunted. Pits still needed horse transport and the number of these, excluding the ponies underground varied from 42 to 37. It cost £57 6*s*. 7*d*. a year to feed one of them in 1874, but this expense tended to decline in the later years of the century. Lord Lilford's income was suffused with the splendour of a prince's revenue. He drew royalties in 1878 of £8,355; by 1888 it was £11,366, figures which were based by the leases on a fixed rent per annum plus a tonnage payment. Arthur John Fletcher was in time to enter the Church and in 1892, the year of his marriage, £5,000 part share of his in the pits was brought into settlement for the benefit of his marriage. The four Fletcher partners in 1888 were Ralph J. Fletcher, George Fletcher, Jane Fletcher and Arthur John, but a new name had been added in 1886, that of Abraham Burrows, who put £5,439 into the partnership in 1886. Unique almost among 19th-century coal masters the Fletchers had been well to the fore in promoting the welfare of their workfolk. In 1908 they built new mess rooms and lavatories and a few years later baths at a cost of £2,000. In 1912 in their company accounts appears a new item, national insurance contributions on the part of the employer. In the workings underground the cost of the ponies was kept distinct from the surface horses and colts. In 1874 in five seams the total cost was considerable at £1,465 4*s*. 10*d*. Boat transport was still a factor and in 1884 a depreciation of £50 a year was allowed for the barges in use, repairs cost £8 12*s*. and interest on boat loans £7 10*s*. Just before the entry of Burrows there had been a breakdown of the value of the shares of the partners. This was in 1885. The shares are given as: Mrs. Katharine Isabella Fletcher, £23,527; George Fletcher, £5,000; Arthur John Fletcher, £13,000; Jane Fletcher, £13,000; Ralph Fletcher and Philip Fletcher together £23,336; total £77,961.

## ST. GEORGE'S SCHOOL, 1873

The school originally in Bag Lane was built in that time, when school building was becoming urgent in Atherton, for between the 1871 census and 1881 the population soared ahead from 7,531 to 12,602, the greatest forward leap it made in any single decade last century or this. The school opened with only 16 scholars on February 24, 1873, with Harriet Bertha Partington as mistress. But constant need for expansion caused a new school for infants to be erected in 1915 under the separate control of M. Chappell, who left in 1924. The old buildings were abandoned in 1936 for new premises on a 1.8 acre site in Derby Street built at the expense of Clement Fletcher, which school so flourished that four new classrooms had to be joined on and in 1969 the façade was remodelled and a kitchen added. F. Nuttall appointed head teacher in 1963 carries historically a dual distinction. He was the first master of the school and is one of a few in the county area admitted, as many of the early free and grammar school masters were, to holy orders. The combined roll of both schools in 1970 was 721, a steady and impressive growth from its foundation in 1873.

## SACRED HEART SCHOOLS, 1875

Margaret Larkin, first mistress, opened the school July 1873 with one unqualified assistant to help out. Until 1950 the buildings were called St. James, but after that the old name was revived. Constant growth in numbers caused new extensions in 1888 and 1909. A fine airy new school with ample playing space was built for the infants in 1960 in Lodge Lane. In 1913, under Anna Whitehead, the average roll was 256 and for the infants division 107. Nora Haugh was teacher for a long period this century and both she and Mrs. Lyon (the married name of Miss Whitehead) consolidated the fortunes of the two schools by loyal and devoted service. Mrs. Lyon taught for 43 years. A sister, Violet Tinker, and two nieces, Florence and Margaret Rush, were associated with these schools, as assistants and head; they were relatives of Joseph Tinker, who sat as M.P. for Leigh from 1923 to 1945.

## THE SELBY FAMILY, 1874

Selbys basked in local prominence from about 1870 to 1916; they filled a role in township affairs similar to that of the Hodgkinsons earlier in the same century. In 1874 John Selby was at Platt Fold and Millin Selby at Atherton Hall. Two years later John D. Selby and Arthur Selby are located at Atherton Old Hall. Millin Selby, born in 1799, died in 1870, was for thirty years the agent of the Lilfords in Atherton, discharging all the duties of the ancient stewards. He was followed by Atherton Thomas Selby, 1835–95, who at one time was invited to manage the Astley Hall estate to try and stave off bankruptcy. Upon his death his second son, John Baseley Selby, succeeded and to the year 1916 managed the growing complexity of his office so that, in all, three generations of Selbys discharged the ever-widening responsibility of stewardship for the absent Lilfords. Edward Selby, fifth son of Atherton Thomas, was a graduate of Cambridge. Another member of the family was Richard Selby, who was a teaching member of University College, Cardiff, and who died in 1942.

## A NEW CHAPEL, 1875

Growth of new industrial populations attracted the presence of strange religious groups who, like the Swedenborgians, congregated and by self-sacrifice hired rooms and later built some place of worship, where they could meet. In Flapper Fold Lane the Progressive Christian Church built a chapel, which was opened June 26, 1875, by the Rev. W. Leask, D.D., of London. These sectarians believed in most of the Christian principles, but the doctrine of eternal punishment disturbed their meditations. They rejected it. The Atherton chapel had a chequered career and ceased as a centre of worship in 1893.

## FLETCHERS OF ATHERTON

The Fletchers originated from Bolton, where the much-scattered family had long been identified with the coalfields. In 1860 Thomas Fletcher was mining in Ainsworth, when right above his tunnels Rylands made a reservoir for his mill. It burst and flooded all the workings. The costly litigation which had to follow established the principle of absolute liability for anything dangerous which a man might bring on his land.

Fletchers were prominent and foremost in Atherton township life for the major part of the 19th and 20th centuries. John Fletcher was a son of Jacob Fletcher; he came to Atherton in 1768 to sink two shafts. He was succeeded by his son Ralph, who besides his coalmines in Atherton had an interest in Ladyshore colliery at Bolton. There was a son, John Atherton, who built up his family's prosperity with the Lovers Lane pit. The corporate name of the company at this time as revealed in the trade directories was John Fletcher and Others. It was this energetic John who sank the Victoria Pit in 1850 and the Volunteer Pit in 1860. About this period James, a brother of John, was general manager. As time progressed the family had to acquire real estate, which was inseparable from mining and a farm was purchased known as Hindles at Howe Bridge. Ralph Fletcher was the outstanding member of the family and from 1867 to 1878 stood at the control of an ever-expanding production of six separate pits. In 1875, to ease the burden of management, Abraham Burrows was admitted in partnership, but Fletchers owned the greater part of the estimated capital. John Seacome Burrows was agent of the firm's group of mines from 1878 to 1900, when Leonard R. Fletcher continued to the year of his death in 1916. Clement then began that long association with the Atherton pits, which covered a period of 45 years. From his experiences of the Pretoria explosion in 1910, he was moved to urge on the building of Mines Rescue Stations as some safeguard against the impact of such dreadful disasters. Ralph Fletcher was not only remarkable for building up the prosperity of his company, but he was the patriarch of a family of individual achievement. He educated his children at Rossall and Oxford. One son, Dennis, became vicar of Swinton. Another, Frank, was headmaster of Marlborough School 1903–11 and of Charterhouse 1911–35. He was knighted in 1937. Leonard Ralph Fletcher was the husband of Katharine Mary Fletcher, the first woman chairman of Atherton District Council and whose work as a county councillor for Lancashire historically sets her public service side by side with the great offices of the state and shire filled by the early Athertons. Fletchers were always supporters of the established church. They built Howe Bridge church and deliberated in the assemblies of convocation. K. M. Fletcher herself was a daughter of A. E. Stocks, once archdeacon of Leicester. She died a widow in 1966. Another son of patriarch Ralph was Ernest, who served with the Manchesters in Gallipoli, Egypt and France and who died a bachelor in 1937. The only daughter of Ralph was Agnes Mary. Schooled at Lady Margaret Hall, Oxford, she became M.A. in 1922. A while she lived at Ambleside with her father but returned to Atherton to her brother James. In 1922, when Clement Fletcher became widower she lived at Hindles Cottage to the year 1930, when both took up residence at Atherton Hall. She died in 1971.

## THE VOLUNTEERS, 1883

Lord of the manor and all the undertenants bore the heavy duty of military service in Atherton, but with the passage of time the obligation became archaic. But there had to be something to replace it. The Lilfords served as officers in the army and in the Northampton yeomanry. In Atherton the Fletcher family saw encouragement of local volunteers as a substitute for the old service of national defence, which had severed itself from the holding of land. There was formed a group of volunteers, who met in the Volunteer Hall, built to provide a meeting place for their activities. A coalpit was named in their honour, where in 1862 a single cob of coal 12 tons weight was hewn and wound up to the surface. An inn, the Volunteer, also came into existence and here the riflemen could meet. In 1883 the Volunteer Hall was built where social functions and assemblies were held. As early as 1859 the corps in Atherton had been founded.

## HINDSFORD AND ATHERTON CO-OPERATIVE SOCIETY, 1886

The co-operative movement of the Rochdale pioneers inspired a small group of working men from Leigh to copy their example and draw up rules for trading on a new basis, the elimination of profit. Leigh Friendly Society prospered and established many shops in Atherton. In 1886 some ten enthusiasts met in Hindsford church school and negotiated for the tenancy of a shop in Lord Street. In this unspectacular way began the Hindsford Mutual Co-operative Society, which later dropped its adjective and called itself the Hindsford and Atherton Co-operative Society. The early secretaries were part-time until the appointment of Thomas

Lyon, who continued in office to 1917, when Samuel Johnson came to succeed him. Under him the society became one of the most prosperous in Lancashire with a membership of nearly 7,000. It was always a real force for good, supplying food cheaply, paying profits back to the members and helping many to acquire their own homes. But prosperity is an elusive and fickle estate. The rise of supermarkets dominated the years of the second world war and to survive Hindsford Society was obliged to close many branches and join with the Bolton and District Co-operative Society. It was significant that this democratic trading venture took such strong root in the subtownship, then the most intensely industrialized district of the whole neighbourhood.

## CHURCH OF ST. MICHAEL AND ALL ANGELS, HOWE BRIDGE, 1877

This church designed by Austin and Paley of Lancaster was consecrated February 8, 1877, by the bishop of Manchester, who was entertained and received by John Fletcher. The building cost £7,000. Its second curate was T. Jackson Smith, who left a year after to become vicar of Bedford in Leigh. His successor was William Robert Clayton. In 1895 the value of the living was returned at £198. Clayton remained at Howe Bridge to the year 1913, when G. H. Jeudwine followed. He in turn came to be succeeded by W. H. Bass. An outstanding vicar was Prosser, who became suffragan bishop of Burnley. In his promotion he emulated Atherton Rawsthorne who at the beginning of this century was bishop of Whalley. Skelton left in 1955 for Walton in Liverpool and later went to South Africa. The advowson of this church vests in three trustees.

## MARMADUKE CHARLES FRANKLAND, 1888

An outstanding figure of his day, he died at the Laburnums. He came to Chowbent chapel in 1852 and was a native of Leeds, born 1815 and trained at Manchester College, York. It is to his credit that at the annual town's meeting in 1872 he moved the adoption of the Libraries Acts of 1855 and 1871. But he failed to get his motion carried. In education he was likewise outstanding and in 1861 enlarged the chapel school and began a day school in 1870. It was at Christmas of 1877 that he was presented with a purse of £133 after 25 years of service. In the history of the chapel this was in historic perspective a renewal of those many acts of appreciation which were so frequently shown between chapel community and chapel minister in the great days of the Woods.

## A GREAT SENSATION, 1878

George Henry Evans was a surgeon fascinated by the diverse applications of that new source of energy and power, electricity. He lived at Avenue House, then part of Atherton as tenant of Lord Lilford and quite near to the very centre of Leigh. In 1878 he connected by wire Gibfield Colliery to the Bedford Basin of Fletchers' Colleries and spoke over the line, a distance of two and a half miles. The event created a stir in the neighbourhood, for it was the forerunner of stupendous achievements.

## THE CHURCH OF ST. JOHN THE EVANGELIST, 1879

Atherton became an independent parish separate from the mother church of Leigh in 1859. Its new status was an index sign of the growing importance of the township. Many considered the old chapel to be too small and in 1874 a public meeting opened the question of a new and larger church, an idea which was supported by the Fletchers. But Lord Lilford cold-shouldered the suggestion and there was difficulty in securing extra land on the west, which was held on three-lives leases. Eventually these were bought in and the second episcopalian chapel of Atherton was demolished in 1877. The new structure was designed by Austin and Paley, architects of the church at Leigh. Progress was slow in completing the design and Bishop Fraser of Manchester dedicated a part of it, so that it could be used in 1879. The original plan was for a turret, but later opinion favoured a tower. The fourth Lord Lilford laid the cornerstone in 1891 and placed the last stone in position in 1890. The cost of the entire ambitious plan was £24,000. Two years later a new organ was installed in memory of Ralph Fletcher, who had died in 1886.

## POPULATION IN 1880

A count of the number of inhabitants of the entire township in 1877 gave a number of 10,450. But the enumerators excluded the 180 inmates of the workhouse, which was situated in Atherton. The same estimation was followed in 1880. The numbers then had grown to 11,975, excluding 267 in the poor law institution.

## THE MINERS' STRIKE, 1881

Chronic unrest in the coalfields produced this great stoppage, which lasted eight weeks. Great numbers of strikers thronged the narrow streets of Leigh and authority, entrenched behind its bulwark of privilege, grew apprehensive of violence. Two magistrates, Jabez Johnson of Pennington and Abraham Burrows of Atherton, read the Riot Act of 1714 at the foot of the obelisk in Leigh Market. The crowd was called upon to disperse, whereupon the protesters left for Atherton. The expense to the rates for the cost of calling in the military to preserve peace was £700.

## ST. ANNE'S CHURCH, HINDSFORD, 1884

Hindsford was constituted an independent parish, June 26, 1884. Early worshippers had built a mission on Swan Island, but succeeding years brought such increase in population and industry that it was resolved to build a fitting new church on a site made attractive by the completion of the direct road to Tyldesley. Mrs. Lee of Alder House laid the foundation stone in 1889 and the fabric was completed in 1901. It cost £9,000. The value of the living was then £210. It was decided to choose St. Anne, the mother of the Virgin Mary, as dedicatory Saint. Her patronal feast falls on July 26. Messrs. Austin and Paley, who designed so many churches in Manchester and other dioceses, were the architects. The old vicarage in Lodge Road was for some time the residence of the vicars of Tyldesley. It was demolished in 1960, when the present vicarage replaced it.

## POLITICAL PARTIES, 1889

Members of the house of Atherton were summoned to Parliament on several occasions; it was a duty which fell their way and they represented the county in the high politics of the realm. One was member for the borough of Liverpool. At first only freeholders could vote; then came the great reform of 1832 and later the wide extension of the right to vote. Dense population in various parts of the kingdom created new divisions and with the making of Leigh constituency in 1885 a political awareness became evident in the old townships. The parties built clubs to draw and keep the allegiance of restive voters. In Atherton the Conservative club began in 1889. The Liberals followed with their premises in 1894, created as a public company from their funds at a cost of £1,500. During this century the rise of a third party occasioned the beginnings of the Labour club. Their first location was in a shop in Market Street in 1921. Later premises near Church House were taken and on January 26, 1961, the present club was opened by the member for Leigh division, Harold Boardman.

## ATHERTON MARKET TOLLS, 1889

Under the control of the house of Lilford were the ancient fairs and markets; once they were held twice a year, but with population growing, the holding of a market became a weekly affair. Much trouble arose over dues and receipts and in 1889 the local board bought out the prescriptive right of the Lilfords. From that time the profits and control over the market have belonged to the local council. In the transfer the market rights were described as market fair tolls, stallages, pickages with the town bell, bell dues, charges for billposting, right to appoint the bellman and the billposter, and other emoluments. Previously all these had been leased to the local board for 21 years. These sources of profit directed into the large Lilford purse were as varied and colourful as they had been in ancient times, when frankpledge, goods of felons, court fines, treasure trove and beggars' cloaks who died in Atherton provided a casual windfall for the Atherton family.

## THE BURROWS FAMILY OF ATHERTON

Abraham Burrows came into Atherton from Liverpool, where he was a journeyman tailor. He changed his livelihood and became a coal agent. He bought stocks from Fletchers at fixed contract prices and, during the Franco-Prussian war, was able to sell at a substantial profit. Later he came to live in Atherton and was one of the first elected councillors to the new local board in 1864. For a time he lived at Green Hall and died in 1901. Burrows prospered at a fast rate; he was in the Howe Bridge mills and entered into partnership with the Fletchers. By contrast to this family, the Burrows were mainly baptist. A son, Miles Formby, managed the great mills at Howe Bridge and was even chairman-director of Fletchers Burrows, when this company became limited. The Baptist chapel owed much to this family—the organ, pulpit and financial aid in many appeals. The sons of Miles were Robert, Miles and William. Robert entered a wider sphere of public service and sponsored the growth of holiday camps to bring together public school boys and boys of working class in state schools. In 1934 he entertained the Duke of York at Bonis Hall, Prestbury, and was knighted in 1937. He died in 1964.

## THE MURDER AT 29 MARKET STREET, 1889

A youth, Walter Davies, was manager of a pawnshop. On July 22 his employer, John Lowe, found him dying on the cellar floor with a deep knife wound in his neck. The motive was robbery and four watches were missing. Suspicion fastened itself on a man from Blackburn who was arrested, but who was able to establish his innocence. The actual murderer proved to be William Chadwick, who was tried at Liverpool Assizes, found guilty and hanged April 15, 1890.

## ST. RICHARD'S SCHOOL, 1891

The opening day of this school in Mayfield Street was April 6, 1891. There was one mistress and one assistant for 126 children. Early struggles which beset this school cannot be recorded, because the first log-book was stolen. Township prosperity pushed on its good fortune and new expansion had regularly to be provided to satisfy the rising intake. There are now 370 scholars on the roll and to meet this increase in numbers a new building was erected on the Flapperfold housing estate with four classrooms.

## THOMAS LEE, 1895

He was a cotton spinner and doubler, active before 1861 in Atherton. Lee Street is named after him. For a time he is to be traced at Alder House and both he and his wife supported good causes within the township, especially in the rapidly expanding Hindsford. He was so prominent a citizen that he was invited to lay the foundation stone of the new church of St. John on April 22, 1878. Another memorial to him was the Dan Lane cotton mill, which eventually became a unit, like the Ena, of the Fine Spinners and Doublers. From the style of the mill structure, it would appear to belong to the age of the 1840s. In the prosperous period of 1881 extensive additions were made but decline set in after the war of 1939–45 ended and the whole mill was dismantled.

## THE FOURTH LORD LILFORD, 1896

He bore the name of Thomas Littleton Powys and like his father went to Christ Church, Oxford, from Harrow. He married twice; his second wife was a daughter of Baillie Hamilton, governor of Newfoundland. He died at Lilford Hall in 1896. The rent roll of this fourth lord in 1883 was £26,398 and the grand total of the acreage of estates in Lancashire and Northants was 15,554. His main interest was ornithology and from the study of birds in his Lilford aviaries he compiled his magnificent *Birds of the British Isles*. He was succeeded by his son John Powys, who died in 1940. Among his bird items were two eggs of the Great Auk.

## BOUNDARY TRESPASS, 1899

Saxon surveyors had marked out the extent of each township that made up the ancient parish of Leigh. These boundaries remained fixed till the 20th century. To change them meant disturbance of rights and dues; feudal law made them virtually impossible to change and the settlement involved in the poor law more difficult still, The fixity yielded to the strains of population and when Leigh was incorporated in 1899 a valuable area of Atherton in the very centre of the new borough was detached. It was an area which had more affinity with Leigh, but it contained over 2,300 people and had potential value in growth of rateable revenue. But there was no way of meeting the problem other than by cession and the boundary of Atherton was pushed back from the Avenue to Orchard Lane. Leigh had to pay compensation of £350 for twenty years. Other pressures exerted their influence in the field of education, when in order to provide sites suitable under modern requirements the Fred Longworth school was built in Hindsford along Printshop Lane, and a second time in 1969, when the Leigh Church of England school was sited in Atherton on Leigh Road.

## A NEW ROAD, 1899

From Tyldesley towards Chowbent the old road meandered across Chanters valley turned sharply in the direction of the Hillock and joined up with Millers Lane. In 1899 the new high-level Tyldesley road was constructed to afford a direct and straight access from Hindsford to Atherton. The old road became a quiet backwater and Chanters farm was thrown into isolation in the valley below.

## SOUTH LANCASHIRE ELECTRIC TRACTION AND POWER COMPANY, 1900

Incorporated in 1900, the company had a capital of £850,000 and its registration name describes adequately what were its objects. It supplied traction or communication by that new source of energy, electricity, and the same power for lighting to both Atherton and Tyldesley townships and street lamps as well. At first there had been two companies, the South Lancashire Tramways and the Lancashire Light Railways, but these now combined to make a major company and build a network of lines to link all the towns in the area which by Act of Parliament they had authority to do. The first directors came from Liverpool and one of these, Arthur Stanley, was a member of the Derby family. In this way trams appeared on the streets of Atherton, single tracks for most of the way, with loops to allow passings. A generating station had to be built near the sheds at Howebridge to supply the power to drive the trams and light the lamps in houses and on the roads. These trams continued to the year 1931, when a new type of pneumatic-tyred vehicle called the trolley-bus gained favour. But the petrol bus soon outstripped all its rivals; it could travel faster and along roads where there were no cables overhead. The company changed its name to the Lancashire United Transport and by its fleet of buses has been a powerful factor in the urbanization of the entire area over which it had powers to operate.

## THE INNS AND TAVERNS OF ATHERTON

Surviving records spanning many centuries sift the historic inns of Atherton from those of comparative new life, which arose during the 19th century. Spinner's Arms, Queen's Arms, Lion, and Station Hotel came into being by reason of the new Bolton Road. The Blue Bell was once the popular name of the Station. At Bridge Foot has stood the Rope and Anchor from long before 1850, when Thomas Gibson was there. And in Market Street Mountain Dew, Jolly Nailor, and at Lane Top the Letters Inn are unfamiliar names till the 19th century approaches, when to meet the demands of a populous community many new premises were licensed: the Volunteer, Bay Horse, Concert Inn, Railway Inn, Albion, Oak Tree Root and Gardener's Arms. Around the parish church many historic inns, which once played some quite distinctive part in township life, have silently faded out, victims of the pressures of a changing age and taste. The Queen's Head, Swan, Bull's Head, Bear's Paw and Rising Sun no longer stand on locations familiar to the ghostly travellers of the old turnpike roads.

## CIVIC BUILDINGS, 1900

A hall called the Court Chamber upon the Chowbent in 1616 was the private property of the Athertons and Irelands. It was a kind of Town Hall, where business relative to the good order of the neighbourhood was carried out. Later matters of quite grave import were debated in the old Chowbent Chapel or at one of the old inns or in the Lane Top schoolroom. After the making of Bolton New Road about 1839 a public hall and news room was built for the better convenience of townsfolk and to meet the need of a growing community. Officials like Edward Manley worked from here and it was here that the first councillors of the 1864 local board came after their election. But in 1900 a new Town Hall, built with Accrington brick and clock tower, occupied the old site and has served town and people in a variety of useful ways during the whole course of the 20th century.

The year 1902 saw the opening of the Baths in Mayfield Street. They cost £5,275, but since larger sums of money than the original outlay have been spent in modernization. The most noteworthy civic building is Formby Hall, presented by the Burrows family in 1916. It serves a great number of purposes and is widely used for civic functions. The changed attitudes of society towards many of the social problems created by dense urbanization led to the building of hostels with warden service and other needful facilities for aged people. Atherton never possessed almshouses in the past. In this way Blakeborough House, so called in commemoration of a clerk of the local council, and Hindsford House arose to meet the needs of aged persons, where in the eventide of life they can pass their days in care and comfort.

## JOINT STOCK BANKS

Townsmen in Atherton had little scope for investment of surplus cash. They lent to neighbours and after the foundation of the Bank of England in 1694 they bought Government annuities. Most banks in their early history were private institutions. Agent Hodgkinson deposited Lord Lilford's rents in a Manchester bank, Jones Loyd and Co. From the Bewsey estate receipts, he lodged these with the bank of Parr, Lyon and Greenhall in Warrington, Banking has been the subject of continual mergers and with the growth of industry in Atherton they became an indispensable feature of modern ways of life. Like the inns, they clustered round the ancient market place. The Bank of Bolton appeared in 1880. This changed in control and at one time the large banks of Williams Deacon's, Westminster and District had branches in the Market Place, succeeding the ancient taverns, where much of a similar type of business had formerly been transacted. In fact one of them occupies the site of the Queen's Head. Competition has continued the process of amalgamation and Westminster, District and National have merged. This branch, dating from 1901, was the old Parr's Bank and the London County. The Union Bank of Manchester in Market Street became part of Barclays in 1940. The latest comer is the Leigh Trustee Savings Bank, first begun in 1932.

## CINEMAS

The great invention of animated pictures on film made its first impact on the masses of industrialized parts of the country early in the 20th century. Itinerant showmen came, set up tents and exhibited to curious crowds, and then went on to the next town. From silent animation with captions evolved the talkies. Atherton gave its patronage over a half century to three houses, the Gem, Savoy and Palace. With the spread of the new medium of television these had to close and their sites were redeveloped for other purposes. In 1924 a picture-house called the Eagle exhibited films in Market Street, while the Gem in Bullough Street called itself the Gem Electraceum.

## ATHERTON PUBLIC LIBRARY, 1905

A lending library had been supported by the Gwillyms at Leigh church in 1750; books were bought and enrolled members paid subscriptions to allow of stock growth. Chowbent chapel trustees collected a number of books, which circulated in the town and minister Frankland tried to get the ratepayers to adopt the Free Library Acts. He failed, but a service was later begun in the public hall, with that many-sided officer, E. Manley, as librarian.

The room was opened on Thursday evening only. Manley was nuisance inspector, school attendance officer, librarian, and chief of the local fire brigade in 1890. To mark in a suitable way the jubilee of the Queen's accession in 1897 the town voted to adopt the Library Act and establish this rewarding service. With the Carnegie grants it was possible to speed on the project and the present building was opened by Lord Lilford on May 24, 1905. Gervase C. Briars was the librarian from the opening year to 1945.

## COTTON SPINNING MILLS, 1905

The early years of the 20th century saw the rise of many independent spinning units built and floated in Leigh and Atherton. Laburnum number one mill dates from 1905 and the second from 1907. The name derives from a house now no longer standing, where it was planned to build. In 1908 the Ena mill off Gloucester Street began its trading life, the name said to be in honour of a regent queen of Spain. The capital of Ena was £80,000 in coupon shares of £5. In the 1920 boom these companies were over-capitalized; this hampered their prosperity later in an export field which was being dangerously assailed by foreign competition. The Ena joined with Shaw Jardine & Co. to weather the storm. They changed the name to "E" mill and later, as a unit of Fine Spinners, the concern was absorbed by the giant Courtaulds. Laburnum Mills was forced into the Combined English Mills and later Viyella, which organization was taken over by Imperial Chemical Industries Ltd.

## THE OLD HALL MILL, 1909

Atherton had two manorial mills worked by water and dam race from the brooks. They were the signs of manor status for the Lodge and Atherton Hall. All trace of the Lodge mill has long since gone. When steam began to be applied as a power of industry, the steam engine ousted the water mills, which could not function in frosty weather or in drought. In 1909 there was a steam engine grinding corn at Old Hall Mill; John Harrison was the miller, genial and obliging to all who gave him custom.

## THE PRETORIA DISASTER, DECEMBER 21, 1910

The dreadful explosion at the Pretoria Pit is part of Atherton history in that 28 of the total number of 333 dead were from Atherton. The tragedy occurred at ten minutes to eight in the morning, when an accumulation of firedamp gas was ignited by a spark from a faulty electrical cable in the Yard mine. The blast was so terrific that the flames travelled up the tunnel way and shot into the shaft of the pit with such force that part of the headgear was destroyed and descent and ventilation by this access became impossible.

## CENTRAL PARK, 1912

Industrial communities need relaxation and one way is to provide parklands and open spaces. Central Park was made in 1912 on land leased from Lilford covering 10 acres and subject to a rent of £56 15*s*. per annum. Spaces in Lodge Lane and Devonshire Place are found in other parts of the township. When the cotton industry declined and with it the numbers engaged in the mills, it became difficult to maintain the Howe Bridge Welfare grounds. These extended to over 10 acres, which the urban council in 1963 acquired for £21,800.

## BURTONS OF HINDSFORD, 1913

James Burton and his sons made industrial history by their great cotton mills, which near Shakerley Brook bestrode the boundaries of Tyldesley and Hindsford. One of his several mills was called Atherton Mill and another Lodge Mill. The buildings in Tyldesley were all demolished in the great depression of the 1930s, but later-built factories in Hindsford were sold to an electrical firm of Ward and Goldstone. Edward Burton was one of the first elected councillors of Atherton in 1864. He became fabulously wealthy and purchased an estate in Denbighshire. Fred Burton succeeded to the ownership of this extensive Welsh property and died in 1913, a millionaire. To his mountain home there used to come on visit, Beatrix Potter, writer of children's stories, and in her *Journal* she has left a pen picture of Uncle Fred in old age, riding in a ramshackle carriage drawn by an old cabhorse that had bolted several times in the streets of Manchester, and so mean he looked twice at every halfpenny before he parted.

## THE 1914–18 WAR MEMORIAL

No less than 306 sons of Atherton paid the supreme sacrifice in this war, when the machine-gun, like the longbow of old, was the dominant weapon. All except one, Lieutenant Bullough, belonged to the non-commissioned ranks. With the return of peace a memorial in their honour was erected by public subscription on a triangle of lawn where meet two roads, Leigh Road and Hamilton Street. Today it is a reminder of the huge sacrifice of plebeian blood which that war exacted and to the wayfarer with any historic sense it is proof that the great duty of military service placed on all tenants in feudal days under the house of Atherton is still that inescapable and onerous burden in times of national danger.

## JOHN JAMES WRIGHT, 1919

He served his chapel congregation for the wide space of 28 years. In 1891 he came from Bolton to Chowbent and resigned in 1919, when Mortimer Rowe succeeded. In the years of his retirement he wrote an anecdotal history of his famous meetinghouse, which was a pleasant contribution of conventicle reminiscences mixed with what historical fact was then available. It was the first major effort at preserving that priceless treasure of tradition which had grown to be associated with both chapel and township. He issued his *History of Chowbent Chapel* on the occasion of the bicentenary of its foundation. High praise be his, for having enriched the cultural heritage of the place in which he served so well.

## CULTURAL ACTIVITIES, 1920

Atherton township set great store by learning; in no other part of the extensive parish of ancient Leigh was culture so widespread. This has been amply proved by the number of books which testators prized and bought and which they left to after generations almost as heirlooms. Much of this learning was biblical and theological. In 1920 was formed a branch of the Workers' Educational Association in Atherton to help to bring university teaching within the scope of any wishing to learn. R. Wynne Jones was the secretary for 50 years and by his loyal service university teachers came year in year out to impart knowledge on wide and varied subjects. For his outstanding devotion to this democratic form of education he was made M.A. *honoris causa* by the University of Manchester, which was the sponsoring centre for the supply of tutors able to offer subjects in the open field of which they had themselves gained distinction. But Atherton went further in this post-war era. It formed a Literary Society, to appreciate the heritage of former times by arranging meetings and lectures on winter nights. John Bullough and Tom Turner were two who were identified with this worthy grouping.

## HARRISON PARSONAGE, 1925

Ministers of the unitarian chapel have been in their long pastoral history resident in various places. Once they lived in the closest vicinity of the chapel. J. J. Wright occupied a house in distant Old Hall Mill Lane. In 1925 the trustees built a new house along Bolton Road, which was given its distinctive name in honour of a previous minister and his family, benefactors in many ways of the old foundation. Two other manses were provided. The Baptists settled their pastor in a house in Bee Fold Lane in 1924, and in rival emulation the Methodists chose a near site in Hamilton Street for Epworth House. This has been the home of the circuit ministers since 1930.

## ST. RICHARD'S CHURCH, 1927

The foundation stone of this Catholic church was laid on October 1, 1927 by F. W. Keating, archbishop of Liverpool. It stands in Mayfield Street in proximate association with the older schools. Its dedication was in honour of St. Richard of Chichester of glorious memory. Priest and canon, T. A. Almond served here for the long space of 46 years. The Presbytery dates from 1908.

## BRIARCROFT, 1927

Philip Fletcher died in 1927. Briarcroft was his residence along Leigh Road and this he gave to the public for use as a social centre and club. The Fletcher family were always mindful of the welfare of their workfolk and in 1875 had furthered a scheme, which resulted in the building of the Atherton Village Club. The company needed large numbers of miners, but these had to be housed and to meet that need they employed a Dutch architect, who designed rows of cottages in 1873 at both Howebridge and Hindsford. The style difference is striking when contrasted with the traditional local houses erected at the same time. Philip Fletcher was chairman-director of the group of collieries and as colonel reached a rank higher than that of either Ernest or Clement, his brothers. It is strange how this family filled the void left by the absent Lilfords, not only socially, politically and in general public interest, but also in this acquittance of that old feudal duty of military service, which was enforced upon every tenant of Atherton manor. Briarcroft is now the property of the Lancashire County Council.

## TELEPHONE EXCHANGE, 1933

The first telephone call by Evans from Bedford to Fletchers' collieries in 1878 was speedily adapted for industrial purposes by firms in Atherton. The initiative was taken by the National Telephone Company, which before 1900 had set up an exchange in Atherton for commercial and private users. This company established other centres in the dense areas of population, but for intercommunication the caller had to use the lines of the general post office. As the network was inevitably covering the whole of the kingdom, the private companies had to cede to the Post Office monopoly, which today, except for Hull city, is complete. After the end of war in 1918 great progress was made from the early magneto type of apparatus to the general switchboard, which itself has yielded to the automatic. The present exchange was erected in 1933. It is a building of some architectural merit. The change to automatic was in 1964.

## THE 1939–45 WAR

National peril forced on the sons of Atherton the duty of military service for a second time in the 20th century. With the conquest of the machine-gun and the rise of the tank, the casualties in this second conflict for Atherton sank from 306 to 109. But the pattern of losses mostly confined to other ranks remained much the same. Only two lieutenants lost their lives, one, J. D. Hampson in a Tunisian battle, in which a Bolton officer won the coveted honour of the Victoria Cross.

## THE SEVENTH LORD LILFORD, 1950

John Powys, fifth peer, died in 1940 and was succeeded by his bachelor brother, Stephen. He died in 1949 and there was no direct heir to take. It was then found necessary to trace through the pedigree as far back as the second peer and follow through the male line. In this way George Vernon Powys, thrice great-grandson of the second lord, became entitled to the estates and peerage. He is a South African, with a preference for life in that country and lives in Cape Town. He has issue two daughters, born of his fourth marriage. He himself was born in 1931.

## GREENHALL SCHOOL, 1957

This special type of school serving the whole of division 15 of the Lancashire County was erected on a site of nearly 4 acres off Bolton Road and opened by Sir Denys Stocks in November of that year. The school accepts boys and girls who are unequal to make the pace of average instruction as provided by other schools and trains them intensively to be useful members of modern society. The roll numbers on average 120, with a head teacher, a staff of 10 and one nursery assistant.

## THE END OF THE COALPITS, 1966

Cotton and coal had brought boundless prosperity to Atherton. The two were interdependent. The development of the steam engine had made possible a source of power for driving the great mills and these engines, often given individual names, like the Perseverance and Energy of Howe Bridge factories, functioned with remarkably little maintenance over long decades. This same application of tremendous power made deep-seam mining possible and the pits in Atherton raised staggering tonnages. But after the end of the second world war a sharp frost assailed both industries and pits on the Lancashire coalfield closed in rapid succession. Howe Bridge colliery finished in 1957, Gibfield in 1963 and Chanters ended its long life in 1966. Significantly at this final scene of an era of coal J. C. Fletcher saw the last tub brought up from Chanters. For 200 years coal and the Fletcher family had dominated the Atherton stage.

## A BREAK WITH TRADITION, 1966

For 900 years the houses of Atherton and Lilford had a resident representative steward or agent to supervise the local estates. He was that embodiment of the ghostly succession of Cowper, Green, Taylor, the Hodgkinsons and the Selbys, the last of the feudal officers and a memorial of their vanished greatness. In 1966 Jossylyn Alleyne Robinson died. He had been agent for long years. Fragmentation of the estates, large tracts passing into public ownership, closure of the mines, diminished his importance, leaving his successor to break the tradition and move the estates office to Bretherton near Preston. In this way the last of the true manorial officers left Atherton; the wheel of fate, which had placed, as a result of the Norman conquest, both vill and manor in the tenacious grasp of one family was turning against them.

## HESKETH FLETCHER SENIOR SCHOOL, 1967

Staff and scholars, some 700 in all, left the old school at Lane Top in 1967 to occupy new and modern premises in Hamilton Street. The foundation stone had been set by Mrs. K. M. Fletcher in 1965, who herself had filled with distinction one of the most onerous offices of county administration, that of chairman of the education committee. True to tradition the new school was declared open by James C. Fletcher, a son of Clement. Lane Top school in 1840 had been assigned one half-acre. The new school covers with playing fields over 21 acres. And the all-in cost was £330,000.

## CURATES AND VICARS OF ATHERTON

Atherton as a parish was carved out of Leigh, which was a vicarage and so Atherton had to be of that status. When other parishes were created, as in Hindsford and Howebridge, these too were vicarages. Sedgwick was the first perpetual curate. His successor was John Lowe of Trinity College, Cambridge. In time he was succeeded by Thomas Foxley, who held the living for a record 60 years. During the last period of his life, a curate, Ebenezer Booth, did most of the work. Many looked to the next presentation, which Lord Lilford advertised before Foxley had died. The description of the benefice was in flowery language, very good relations with parishioners as there were no tithes to collect, for this caused much unpleasantness. Foxley was said to be 90 years of age and the value of the benefice £130. His lordship asked £500 for the presentation. A lady in Horwich bought it for £450 and Lilford as patron put forward her son, Samuel Johnson, as presentee. He was M.A. of Lincoln College, Oxford. It was during the lengthy stay of Foxley that the small brick edifice was taken down and the second chapel built. This curate was a man of means and once sent £10 to Hodgkinson to relieve distress in Atherton in the 1820s. William Nuttall, of St. Catharine's, Cambridge, came in 1870. His daughter married E. H. Edwardes, one of the builders of the Lancashire United Transport. Of later vicars, Cameron was a Scot and Peel claimed descent from the prime minister. Rosenthal had been archdeacon of Singapore and E. J. C. King-Salter at the end of a military career of distinction trained as an ordinand. Besides the award of the D.S.O., he is also a member of the Order of the British Empire. Wounded in one engagement, he lost a foot. He was instituted in 1957.

## ATHERTON CHURCH HOUSE, 1971

Towards the end of the 19th century many Anglican churches built premises where the youth in attendance at either church or Sunday school could meet for recreation. There were billiards, dances and many other social activities. They were given the name of Church Houses and in time they lost popularity. Atherton built a substantial such house in Dan Lane. It began to incur financial loss and was demolished in 1971.

## THE DRAMA AND THE PLAYERS

The curtain comes down on the local scene and one act of the drama is played. In it first appeared the Romano-Celts in the valley, where they left evidence of their lives in coins; then the lights went out on the dark world of their time and for a millennium there is nothing to tell. A thousand years is a puny part of cosmos creation; the mystery of the great universe still persists and the powerful drama goes on in tireless presentation. Each townsman of Atherton and Chowbent has played his part in one unfolding scene, which began in darkness and forges on into darkness. For be his part great or slight, whether in the forefront or in the wings, destiny has made him an actor of a world theatre, and when he abandons the stage the play still goes on.

Chowbent School adopted the name British and like the old free grammar schools observed Shrove Tuesday as a holiday. By 1866 the numbers had risen to 343 and by 1890 to 433. Barker taught well into the next century and was still active in 1913. In 1962 the school lost its seniors and was given aided status. There are now some 120 juniors enregistered.

## ATHERTON SPINNING COMPANY, 1860

The first mill of this consistently successful concern was built in 1860, with a capital of £50,000 in the then popular coupon of £10. The promoters, whose chairman was Jonathan Hesketh of Two Porches, were John Warburton, Richard Manley, Philip Manley of Manor House, James Ridgway and Robert Cowburn, both in High Street, Peter Greenhalgh and Thomas Peake in the Valley. First meetings were held in the King's Head inn. John Manley was secretary in the early period. Later two other mills were built on land to the rear of the first mill along Bolton New Road. When in 1957 the company ceased as a spinning unit the first mill was taken down and the others adapted to varying purposes. For a long time Fred Isherwood of Tyldesley was a member of the board and H. L. Moulds in active co-operation of its trading fortunes.

## THE THIRD LORD LILFORD, 1861

His name was Thomas Atherton Powys; born in 1801 he was educated in the best traditional manner befitting his rank and lineage at Eton and Christ Church, Oxford. He read classics and graduated in 1824. From 1831 to 1837 he was Lord of the Bedchamber to William IV and Lord in Waiting to the young Queen Victoria from her accession year 1837 to 1841. This third Lord Lilford was a determined opponent of the vicar of Leigh, James Irvine, a tractarian. In 1852 his lordship rode up to the House of Lords to present a petition containing 6,211 names and signatures asking that the vicar be removed from his office. This violent opposition to Irvine resulted in a secession from the parish church and to the building of Christ church in Pennington, where Lord Lilford laid the foundation stone in 1853. Just before his death he inherited one-half of the Bank estate at Bretherton, near Preston, from the Kecks of Leicestershire. The fourth lord acquired the other half by purchase in 1880. By his will he said £30,000 was to be raised out of Atherton estate and £9,999 from Bewsey to provide portions for the younger members of his family. The full amount taken from Atherton was £20,800.

## THE FIRST ATHERTON LOCAL BOARD, 1864

In the previous year townsfolk had met and agreed to adopt the Local Government Act of 1858, which allowed a body of rate-payers to create a local board of popularly elected representatives to oversee the day-to-day business of the township carried out by paid and salaried officials. It was the answer to many of the problems created in south Lancashire by the large increase in population due to the influx of workers needed by industry and who had flocked to the coalfields from all parts of the kingdom. The names of the first elected representatives are listed in an appendix. So arose a democratic body, the forerunner of many urban district councils, destined to carry the ever-growing burden of local government pushed far beyond the scope and financial ability of the manorial courts and the local hustings, which had sufficed to solve the problems of a less complex order of society.

## LABURNUM STREET WESLEYAN CHAPEL, 1865

Though John Wesley had come to Chowbent in 1766, it was not till 1865 that the dissenters came to be identified with a chapel place of their own. J. Hayes in this year laid the foundation stone; he belonged to the Westleigh family of cotton spinners, who had been some of the most fervent of Wesley's followers. Licences had been granted to several ministers to hold meetings in cottages and eventually in this neighbourhood, which was a dense combination of folk and works, where the new religion stood the best chance to root and thrive, a chapel arose. It served the district of its industrial birth to the erection of a new house of prayer on Bolton Road early this century. In 1899 Bolton Road chapel was built, but services continued for some time in the old chapel. Meanwhile Bag Lane worshippers had built their own chapel, in which neighbourhood the independent and primitive methodists had established themselves. The primitives in Alma Street exist no longer. The trustees sold the building, which is now in use as a chapel of rest. Laburnum Street and Bolton Road chapels formed part of the Darwen circuit. Bag Lane by contrast was in the Leigh supply of ministers.

## HOWE BRIDGE MILLS, 1868

The first mill of this great industrial unit was built in 1868; the capital of the company was £50,000 with shares of the usual coupon of £10. There were seven directors; James Pearson Fletcher was made chairman and Abraham Burrows, vice-chairman. In time the company built five other mills; the one known as No. 6 being among the very few erected in the postwar era of 1919, when the cotton industry began its contraction. In that year the entire company was refloated by George Clapperton, who had been associated with the mills all his working life. Ten years later they merged with Combined Egyptian Mills and later joined the Viyella International Group. Mills Nos. 2 and 5 were taken down in 1965.

## SACRED HEART CHURCH, HINDSFORD, 1869

This finely proportioned church arose in this year on a site donated by Lord Lilford and was built to serve the spiritual needs of a great number of workers in mines and mills from diverse and distant parts. John Holland, manager of the Yew Tree Colliery in Tyldesley, arranged for celebrations of mass in a loft behind the Star and Garter inn in Tyldesley. Later the bishop of Liverpool sent a priest, J. Lennon, to help on the growth of a new parish in adjacent Hindsford. Holland gave timber, bricks and other material to build the church, schools and presbytery. Many difficulties arose owing to lack of funds and bad times of trade, but in 1869 Bishop Goss of Liverpool came to consecrate this new house of devotion. The next parish priest, Richard O'Neill, was a man of mark and energy; he erected the old infants school and when able directed his drive to Boothstown and Atherton, where missions were established. His successor was Louis Verbrugge, a Belgian exile, who returned to his war-shattered country during the 1914–18 war. Another priest to follow with distinction was Canon Whiteside, a brother of the archbishop of the diocese.

## HOWE BRIDGE SCHOOL, 1869

It served as a mission for 8 years and opened its doors to 38 young scholars, January 11, 1869. Only one mistress, helped by a pupil teacher, struggled bravely with the problems which harassed her day and time. On June 28, 1870, Josephine Smethurst took charge with Jane Rigby as pupil assistant. The curate, C. J. Nateys, came often to give a few hours help and at times his wife, Mrs. Fletcher jnr. and Mrs. Selby and Miss Hesketh taught needlework. Though the 1871 report says the school was fairly taught, the inspector withheld one-tenth of the grant; which meant the church and the school sermons had to make up the loss. In this year the state grant was £32 12*s*., based at 8*s*. per head on results of good teaching and 6*s*. for attendance. Getting a full register fell to the teacher until in 1888 Manley was made attendance officer to combat truancy. Mary Simpson resigned after 2 years in 1874, unable to earn for the managers any grant at all and her successor, S. A. Royle, struggled to pull the school round. She did, but still the tenth was stopped. With the opening of the church in 1877, problems eased. She left in this year with 96 children on the roll and a master, James Halkyard, came. On his first day he noted the discipline as wretched and the singing horrible. He earned a grant of £71 5*s*. 8*d*. less the tenth. In 1880 came the long mastership—42 years—of Holdsworth Clough, under whom both numbers of scholars and staff grew, reflecting the growth of the sub-township by industrialization. There were 274 pupils and 8 staff in 1888. The school had to be enlarged in 1906. The next year it was reported there were 40 half-timers. E. S. Fear was appointed head teacher in 1922. James Dagnall taught from 1952 to 1970. The school in 1932 lost its seniors to the Hesketh Fletcher School.

## THOMAS SALE, CHAPEL CLERK, 1869

Chapel and parish clerks figure as important personages in the history of the places of worship where they served. They had many duties to oversee; to keep notes of burials, baptisms and marriages and give these to the parson to be written up in the registers. The clerkship at Leigh church was often a source of great trouble and tended to descend from father to son. After 1723 in Atherton there are found two clerks with rival duties. One at Chowbent chapel was Thomas Sale, appointed in 1806 and died in 1869, still in office—record of 63 years. He was the last of his long line of apostolic succession. He served his chapel with a degree of loyalty which was exceptional even in that age, when society was stable. A portrait of him was reproduced by Wright in the history of the chapel.

## ST. PHILIP'S SCHOOLS AND CHURCH, 1870

The older buildings are on Bolton Old Road and were opened for scholastic purposes in 1870. A local name of this school was the Blue Bell school, because of its near location to the old inn of that name. A school in Laburnum Street had been started by the Wesleyans and Charles Haslam appears as master in 1869. Laburnum infants continued to the year 1970, when the scholars were absorbed by the additional space built on to St. Philip's. John Ackers of Daisy Hill laid a stone to mark the event and perpetuate the date 1962. Out of the mission school there came St. Philip's church, opened in 1914. A long-serving teacher of Laburnum Street infants was Hannah Sambrook; C. Hope was the last in charge. The roll of St. Philip's is now over 400 and further extensions have had to be provided.